Home Style Bread Making
With Marian Getz

A Collection of Recipes & Tips for your Electric Bread Maker

Copyright © 2008 Marian Getz
All rights reserved. No portion of this book may be reproduced, stored in a retrieval system, or transmitted in any form by any means, mechanical, electronic, photocopying, recording or otherwise, without written permission from the publisher.

Printed in the U.S.A.

Acknowledgements

My sincere thanks to Wolfgang Puck, who hired me in 1998 as pastry chef even though my resume showed that I had no formal culinary education. You accepted my passion for cooking as a substitute and I will be loyal to you for life for giving me this opportunity. You daily inspire me by being the finest example of leadership, artistry, plain old-fashioned hard work, laughter and a burning desire to truly please people with delicious food.

To Greg, my husband of 25 years, you are my best friend, the love of my life and my own personal comedian. How we were ever blessed enough to find each other and to also work side by side all these years I do not know. You are my favorite person to cook for in the whole world. I would not be where I am today without your loving encouragement.

To my sons, Jordan and Ben, it is a privilege to be your mom and it is the best thing I have ever done. Cooking and laughing with you is both my most cherished memory and is what I most look forward to. You have each taught me that indeed all best things in life are free.

To my parents and siblings David, Janet, Adele and John, we were raised in a tiny village deep in the middle of Africa, in a home dedicated to God first and family second. It was there, where you, with brave humor, endured my early kitchen concoctions. I will never forget the disastrous brownies that you less-than-fondly renamed "stove lids," my penchant for banana bread and for suffering (with muffled laughter) through my Julia Child cheese soufflé experiments. You gave me all the love and encouragement a little girl ever needed.

To my amazing bosses and colleagues from the WP side who keep me inspired. Sydney Silverman, Mike Sanseverino, Arnie Simon, Mark Linduski, Jonthan Schwartz, Phoebe Soong, Debra Murray, Cat Chancey and Estela Serrano. To Hiroyuki "Fuji" Fujino, Steve Richard, Angi Colbert, Alba Suarez and Leo Lacey. Thanks to the cookbook team, Daniel Koren, Chris Davis, Tracy Ferguson and Erica Taylor.

I remember the early days of my culinary career when baking bread was an exhausting yet delicious process. The smell and taste of freshly baked bread is something that all of us enjoy and consider an important part of the meal. Now, my new bread maker and Marian's recipes is all you need to help you make this complicated process unbelievably easy and fun.

For over ten years, Marian Getz has been working with me as the pastry chef at my café in Orlando, Florida. Her passion and dedication to excellence helped her create desserts that became so popular that many customers would come to the café just to order Marian's desserts before enjoying an evening out on the town.

After tasting many of Marian's bread recipes, I urged her to write this cookbook to share her recipes with our loyal HSN customers. I know that you will enjoy them as much as I do. Her recipes are easy to follow, fun to make and absolutely delicious.

I learned long ago, beside my mother and grandmother, one should always put lots of love into baking. Marian does just that, which is evident in this wonderful collection of recipes.

Wolfgang Puck

Table of Contents

Acknowledgements	2
Introduction By Wolfgang Puck	3
Bread Making Tips	6
Source Page	157
Index	158

Quick Breads
Page 66

Yeast Breads
Page 12

Cakes & Frostings
Page 85

Gluten-Free Recipes

Page 113

Jams, Jellies & More

Page 134

Bread Making Tips

These tips will help you make the most out of your bread making experience:

Salt

The salt used in this book is Diamond Crystal Kosher Salt. It is half as salty as most other brands. This is because the grains are very fluffy and therefore not as many fit into a measuring spoon. This brand also lists only "salt" as the ingredient in the box. If you are using a different brand than Diamond Crystal Kosher Salt, simply use half the amount specified in the recipe. Salt plays an important role in bread making. It keeps the yeast from growing too quickly, improves flavor and keeps qualities as well as moisture content in the finished bread.

Vital Wheat Gluten

This is a very important ingredient in many bread machine recipes. Gluten is the concentrated protein part of the flour from wheat and a few other grains. To isolate the vital wheat gluten, a ball of dough is washed in water which removes the starch and leaves the very stretchy gluten behind. This is then dried and milled into a powder. Gluten provides the stretchy structure in baked goods. Adding additional gluten to bread recipes will give a much better, higher rise, improves the protein content in the loaf, improves browning and keeps qualities in the finished bread. It greatly helps in recipes with heavy ingredients such as whole grains or nuts and dried fruits.

Vanilla

I adore vanilla and order both my vanilla extract and vanilla beans from a supplier directly from the island of Tahiti. Tahitian beans and extract are my most favorite. I use both of these in recipes where the vanilla takes center stage in flavor. On the other hand, if vanilla is not the star flavor, like say, in chocolate or lemon pound cake, I use imitation vanilla because it adds the correct taste and aroma as back up to the other, stronger flavors in the recipe and is far less expensive. I am also crazy about an inexpensive imitation flavoring called Magic Line Butter Vanilla Extract. It adds an incredible sweet smell to baked goods. Its aroma reminds me of how a really good bakery smells.

Powdered Milk

Adding powdered milk to yeast breads adds protein without adding liquid and greatly improves the rise, flavor and softness in the finished bread. The lactose in the milk improves the browning or caramelization, which adds flavor as well. It is one of the great secrets to making really good bread in a bread machine.

Citric Acid

Citric acid is a byproduct mainly of the citrus juice making industry. I love using it in my jam recipes. Most recipes call for lemon juice. Because lemon juice has a distinct flavor I think that it competes with the flavor of whatever fruit I am using. Jam recipes have so few ingredients in them that it is important to let the fruit flavor really come through. The acid is very necessary in creating a nice "set" or thickening in the jam though, so do not omit this ingredient. Citric acid is also called sour salt and can be found in the kosher-foods section at grocery stores.

Bread Flour

Bread flour has a higher protein content than all-purpose flour and considerably more than cake flour. The protein is important for structure in the loaf. As a rule, yeast breads will turn out better, with a higher rise and softer interior when made with bread flour.

Diastatic Malt Powder

This is made from sprouted barley and is an excellent source of food for yeast if used in small amounts. A good rule of thumb is 1 teaspoon for every 3 cups of flour used. Non-diastatic malt is the more familiar malt found in shakes and malted milk balls.

Bread Machine Yeast

Bread machine yeast is specially formulated to work in the relatively short time a bread machine operates. I recommend brands labeled as "bread machine yeast" for the recipes in this book.

Higher Altitudes

Because of the lower air pressure at high altitudes, baked goods are able to rise much faster. This creates instability in the loaf and frequent collapses during baking. Baking at high altitudes can be very complex and I strongly recommend contacting the Colorado State University for a set of booklets designed to aid in high altitude baking. Their toll free number is 877-692-9358 and email address is cerc1@ur.colostate.edu.

Removing Your Bread From The Pan

The easiest way to remove baked goods from the bread machine pan is 10-15 minutes of patience. When baking is complete, remove the pan from the machine and let it rest for 10-15 minutes. Using a kitchen towel to protect your fingers, gently reach under the pan and turn each wing nut back and forth. Invert the pan onto a plate then invert the loaf back onto another plate, cooling rack or serving tray. If the kneading paddles are inside the loaf, carefully turn it onto its side using a kitchen towel. Use the paddle removal tool to slip the hooked end inside the paddle opening and pull gently. Use caution because the paddles will be very hot. Buttering or spraying the pan before baking does not aid in removing the finished bread.

How To Add Additional Baking Time To A Recipe

If you are baking a loaf and would like to add additional baking time, follow these instructions:
Press and hold STOP until the bread maker beeps.
Press MENU and select BAKE.
Press TIME (machine will be set to 10 minutes).
Increase time if desired by pressing TIME.
Press START.

How To Pre-program The Bread Maker Using The CUSTOM Setting

Breads may be baked using the CUSTOM setting which delays the baking accoding to your needs. Make sure that the ingredients are not perishable and that the yeast is separated from the wet ingredients. To program the bread maker for later baking or to customize a recipe you have created, please refer to the bread maker manual.

Gluten-Free Baking

When making gluten free items, it is important to mix the dry ingredients with the gelatin and xanthan gum separately before adding them to the wet ingredients. If you do not, the gelatin and xanthan gum will form hard, gummy clumps that will remain after baking.

Gluten-Free Ingredients

When you take wheat flour out of a recipe due to allergy, it is a difficult task to try to recreate the role that the gluten in the flour has. The elastic structure is missing and to best duplicate it requires a large number of ingredients with each bringing an attribute to the recipe. Substituting rice, tapioca, cornstarch, bean flours replaces the bulk that wheat flour has. Extra eggs and milk provide protein, aiding in loaf structure. Xanthan gum and gelatin are necessary to help create a stretchy structure to mimic what gluten normally provides. Adding a variety of gluten free flours is more desirable than just one as each kind adds a bit towards duplicating what wheat flour offers.

Jams & Jellies

When making jams and jellies, it is very important to measure accurately. If you do not, you are likely to end up with runny syrup rather than a jam. If you want to make these recipes with less or no sugar, try one of the newer types of pectin that are made for this. Jams and jellies may be stored, refrigerated for up to 3 months or frozen for up to 1 year.

Cakes

When you make cakes in the bread machine you will notice that the texture is somewhat heavier and that cakes are not as tall as they would be if made in the conventional way. This is because the bread maker's gentle mixing does not incorporate very much air into ingredients. I am happy to make this sacrifice for the ease the bread maker offers for this type of baking.

Different Bread Maker Models

While this cookbook is written for use with the Wolfgang Puck Digital Bread Maker, you may use these recipes with many other bread maker models. Follow the manufacturer's directions of your bread maker and do not exceed the volume of ingredients your machine can accommodate.

Water Temperature

The water used in the yeast bread recipes should be cold water at room temperature. It is not necessary to warm the water.

Measurements

The most important thing in using your bread machine is accurate measuring. Incorrect measuring can affect the outcome greatly. Other factors that may affect the results of your bread making are the moisture content of the ingredients you use as well as the humidity and temperature of your location. Check your bread as it mixes. If necessary, adjust with a small amount of flour if the dough seems too sticky, or a small amount of water if the dough seems too dry. Here are a few common mistakes that you may encounter:

Problem:	Solution:
Short, hard "hockey puck"	Forgot to add the yeast.
Tall loaf with a deep crater in the top	Added too much liquid.
Gnarled, dry loaf	Added too little liquid.
Bread touched lid while baking	Added too much yeast.
Sides of loaf collapse inward	Added too much sugar and/or liquid.

Please refer to the bread maker manual for more information on troubleshooting.

I recommend these tools to help you achieve perfect results:

Wire Cooling Rack

Dry Measuring Cups

Glass Liquid Measuring Cup

Off-Set Bread Knife

Measuring Spoons

Pastry Brush

Silicone Spatula

Yeast Breads

Brioche	13
Easiest White Sandwich Bread	14
All-American Wheat Bread	16
100% Whole Wheat Bread	18
Seven Grain Bread	20
Home Style Buttercrust Bread	22
Challah	24
Pumpernickel Bread	26
English Muffin Bread	28
French Bread	30
Chili Cheese Bread	32
Easy Very Cheesy Bread	33
All-American Hamburger Buns	34
Kalamata Olive Sourdough Bread	36
Kansas Sunflower Seed Bread	38
Focaccia Bread	40
Onion & Sage White Bread	41
Sourdough Teff Bread	42
Sourdough Starter	43
French Bread with Sourdough Starter	44
Old Fashioned Rye Bread	45
Savory Mushroom Bread	46
Sour Cream & Chive Bread	47
Confetti Veggie Bread	48
Pepperoni Pizza Bread	50
Wolf's Pizza Dough	51
Wild Rice Bread	52
Thanksgiving Bread	53
Whole Grain Oatmeal Bread	54
Sweet Potato Bread	55
Brown Butter Sandwich Bread	56
Brown Butter	57
Pistachio Bread	58
Cinnamon Raisin Bread	60
Coconut Yeast Bread	62
Hawaiian Sweet Bread	64
Chocolaty Yeast Bread	65

Brioche

Makes 1 loaf

Ingredients

⅓ cup water
3 tablespoons granulated sugar
3 large eggs
1 tablespoon kosher salt

½ cup (1 stick) unsalted butter, softened
3 cups unbleached all purpose flour
1 tablespoon bread machine yeast

Brioche is a very rich bread. It has an almost cake-like crumb with an intense butter flavor and aroma. The loaf is a deep golden color on the outside and a creamy light yellow on the inside. It contains more sugar and eggs than most other breads. The dough is very sticky and difficult to work with, which is why I am grateful for having a bread machine so I don't have to make it by hand anymore. I love to enjoy a slice of this bread for breakfast with some raspberry jam. Use any leftovers to make French toast or bread pudding. Just before the bread machine starts the baking process (about 1 hour and 50 minutes into the cycle), cut a shallow slit into the top of the dough. This will prevent a crack to form on one side of the top of the loaf during baking.

1. Place all ingredients in the order listed into the bread maker; close lid.

2. Press MENU and select BASIC.

3. Press SIZE and select LARGER.

4. Press COLOR and select DARK.

5. Press START.

6. Total machine time is 3 hours.

Marian's Tip:
This is one of the few breads containing yeast where you do not want to use bread flour. Use unbleached all purpose flour for a more tender bread.

Easiest White Sandwich Bread

Makes 1 loaf

Ingredients

1 cup water
1 teaspoon apple cider or white vinegar
1 tablespoon sugar
1 tablespoon kosher salt
¼ cup vegetable oil
3 cups unbleached bread flour
2½ teaspoons bread machine yeast

This basic recipe is made with pantry staples. It is not as tall or showy as some of the other recipes, but it is an old favorite and I make all the time. This bread can best be compared to sandwich bread you can find at the grocery store. It is tasty yet plain enough to let other flavors come through.

1. Place all ingredients in the order listed into the bread maker; close lid.

2. Press MENU and select BASIC.

3. Press SIZE and select LARGER.

4. Press COLOR and select MEDIUM.

5. Press START.

6. Total machine time is 3 hours.

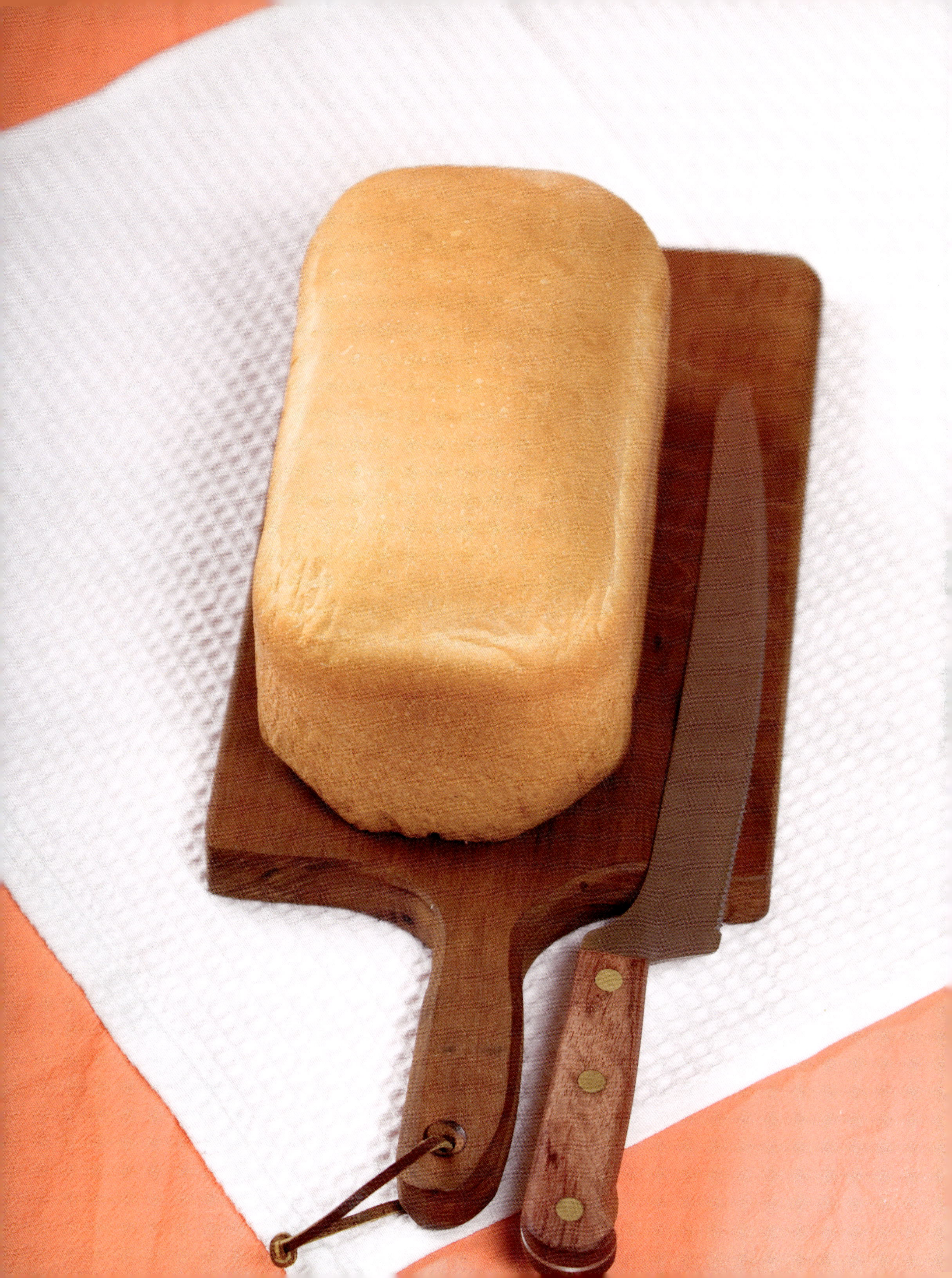

All-American Wheat Bread

Makes 1 loaf

Ingredients

1 cup + 1 tablespoon water
2 tablespoons extra-virgin olive oil
2 tablespoons honey
1 large egg
3 tablespoons powdered milk
1 tablespoon vital wheat gluten

½ teaspoon diastatic malt powder (optional)
1 tablespoon lecithin (optional)
1 tablespoon kosher salt
1 cup 100% whole wheat flour
2 cups unbleached bread flour
2 teaspoons bread machine yeast

A fond reminder of my childhood, I found this recipe in a faded newspaper article tucked between the pages of my sister Adele's old cookbook. This is the wheat bread I remember from my childhood. It is a lighter wheat bread and a cross between white sandwich bread and the healthier whole-wheat loaves we didn't care for when we were little. This combination of flour makes a bread that children love while still providing good nutrition. It is a very tall but tender loaf that is pale on the inside with lovely flecks from the whole-wheat flour. Greg loves this bread as an egg salad sandwich, and this is definitely my idea of a perfect all-American bread.

1. Place all ingredients in the order listed into the bread maker; close lid.

2. Press MENU and select WHOLE WHEAT.

3. Press SIZE and select LARGER.

4. Press COLOR and select DARK.

5. Press START.

6. Total machine time is 3 hours and 40 minutes.

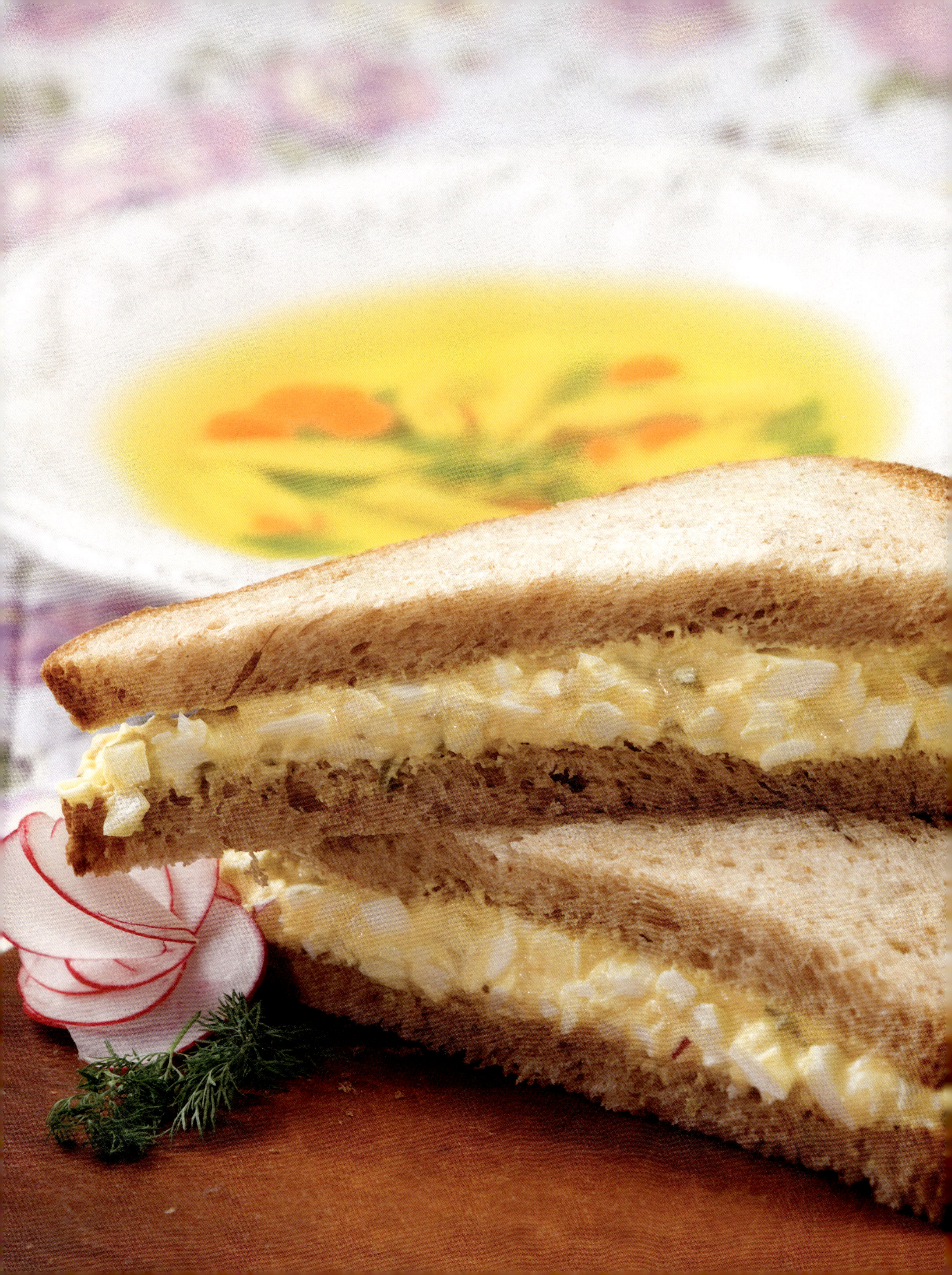

100% Whole Wheat Bread

Makes 1 loaf

Ingredients

1 1/3 cups water
2 tablespoons unsalted butter, softened
1 tablespoon lecithin (optional)
2 tablespoons honey
4 tablespoons powdered milk

4 teaspoons vital wheat gluten
1 tablespoon kosher salt
3 cups 100% whole wheat flour
2 teaspoons bread machine yeast

This 100% whole-wheat recipe is so good that you will love it even if you don't usually eat whole-wheat breads. It is wheaty, moist, and faintly sweet from the honey. It is a very tall loaf with a beautiful crumb. The extra gluten in this recipe gives the heavy whole-grain a lift and makes this bread lighter than other comparable breads. The optional lecithin (made from soybeans) maintains the freshness of this loaf. I use it mostly in recipes that contain more costly ingredients. Lecithin can be found at health food stores.

1. Place all ingredients in the order listed into the bread maker; close lid.

2. Press MENU and select WHOLE WHEAT.

3. Press SIZE and select LARGER.

4. Press COLOR and select DARK.

5. Press START.

6. Total machine time is 3 hours and 40 minutes.

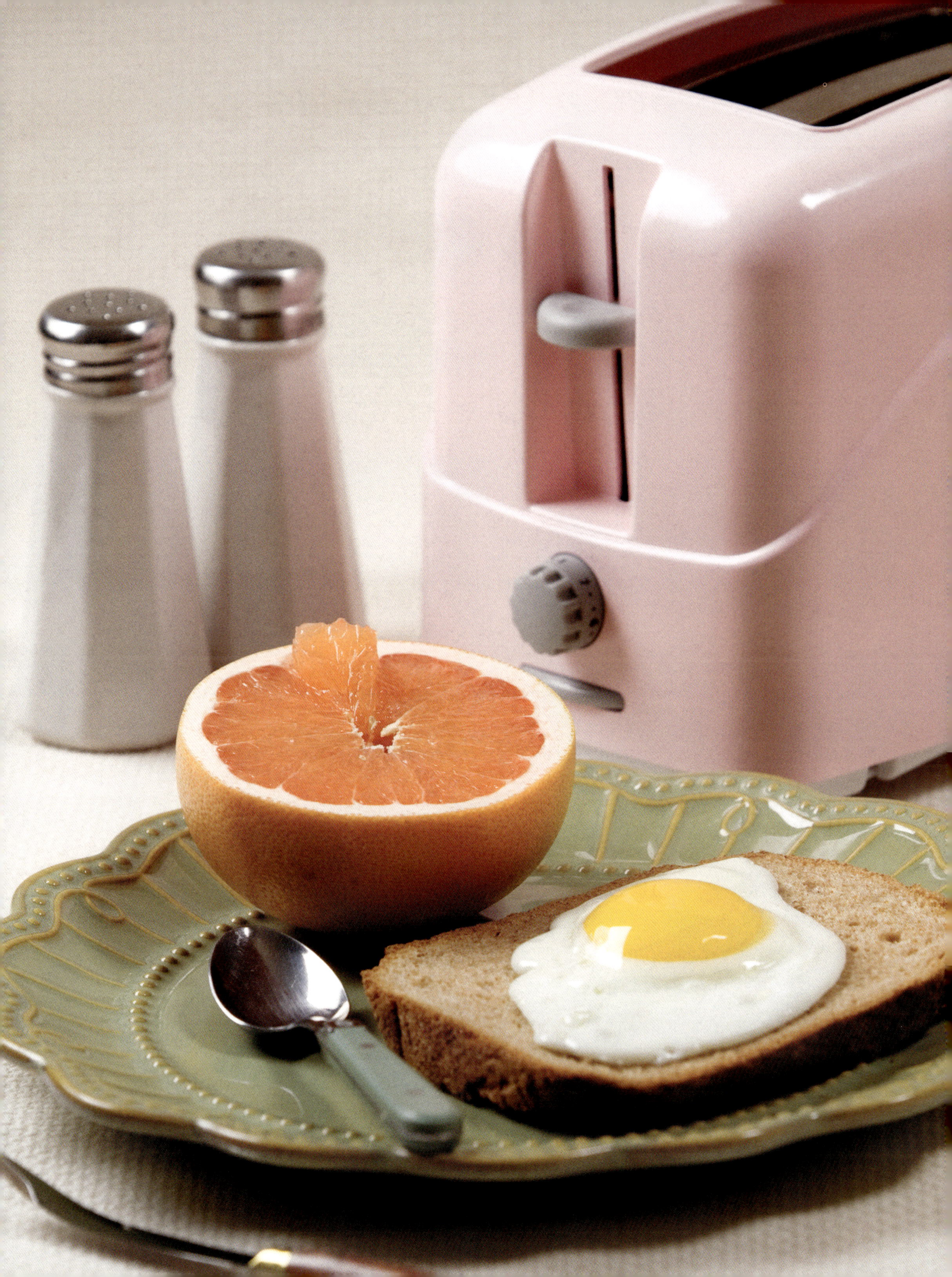

Seven Grain Bread

Makes 1 loaf

Ingredients

1 1/3 cups water
2 tablespoons olive oil
1 tablespoon soy sauce
2 tablespoons powdered milk
4 teaspoons vital wheat gluten

1 tablespoon kosher salt
1 tablespoon granulated sugar
1 cup seven-grain blend**
3 cups unbleached bread flour
1 1/4 teaspoons bread machine yeast

*** Seven-grain blend is a blend you make yourself by combining wheat berries, rye flakes, rolled oats, sunflower seeds, flax seed, poppy seeds and millet.*

Enjoying whole-grains is very easy when they are part of a great tasting bread like this. The easiest place to find these grains is in a health food store where the bulk bins are. Be sure to store these grains in the freezer to preserve freshness and nutrition.

1. Place all ingredients in the order listed into the bread maker; close lid.

2. Press MENU and select WHOLE WHEAT.

3. Press SIZE and select LARGER.

4. Press COLOR and select DARK.

5. Press START.

6. Total machine time is 3 hours and 40 minutes.

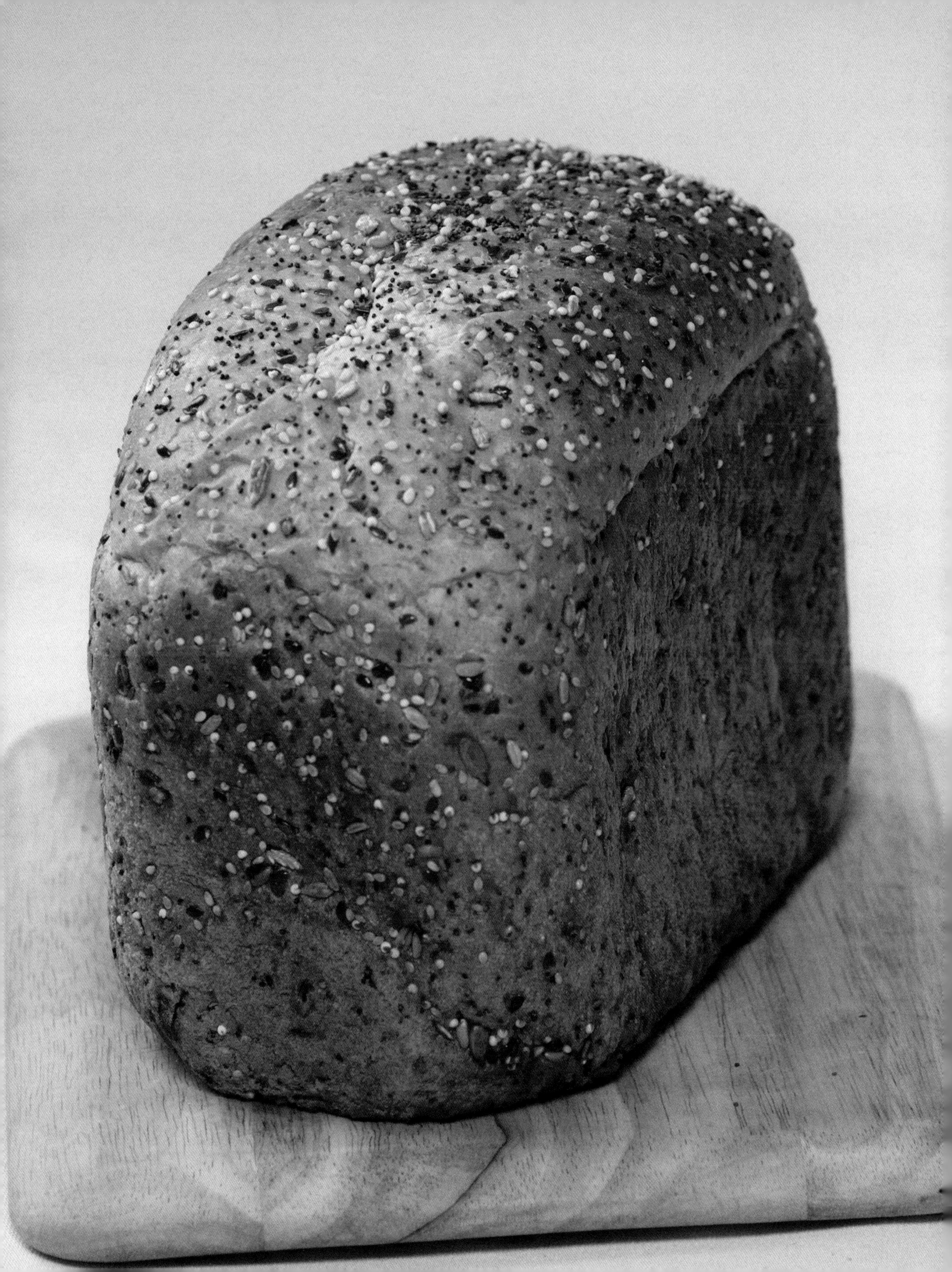

Home Style Buttercrust Bread

Makes 1 loaf

Ingredients

1 cup + 1 tablespoon water
5 tablespoons unsalted butter, softened
1 large egg
2 tablespoons granulated sugar
1 teaspoon diastatic malt powder (optional)

3 tablespoons powdered milk
4 teaspoons vital wheat gluten
1 tablespoon kosher salt
3 cups unbleached bread flour
2 teaspoons bread machine yeast

Growing up in a home where we baked all of our bread from scratch in a old, wood stove, I cannot remember a time when I was anything less than eager to get elbow-deep into the kneading process. I love everything about dough. Nowadays, with my busy lifestyle, homemade bread like that could only be made as a very special treat. That is, until I discovered the bread maker. It is so much easier using this machine. Just dump in the ingredients and enjoy the taste and smell without the effort. This old-fashioned, soft bread is a bit buttery and faintly sweet with a lovely texture that is perfect for a sandwich, toast for breakfast, or, as my family likes best, torn off in chunks right from the machine's pan.

1. Place all ingredients in the order listed into the bread maker; close lid.

2. Press MENU and select BASIC.

3. Press SIZE and select LARGER.

4. Press COLOR and select DARK.

5. Press START.

6. Total machine time is 3 hours.

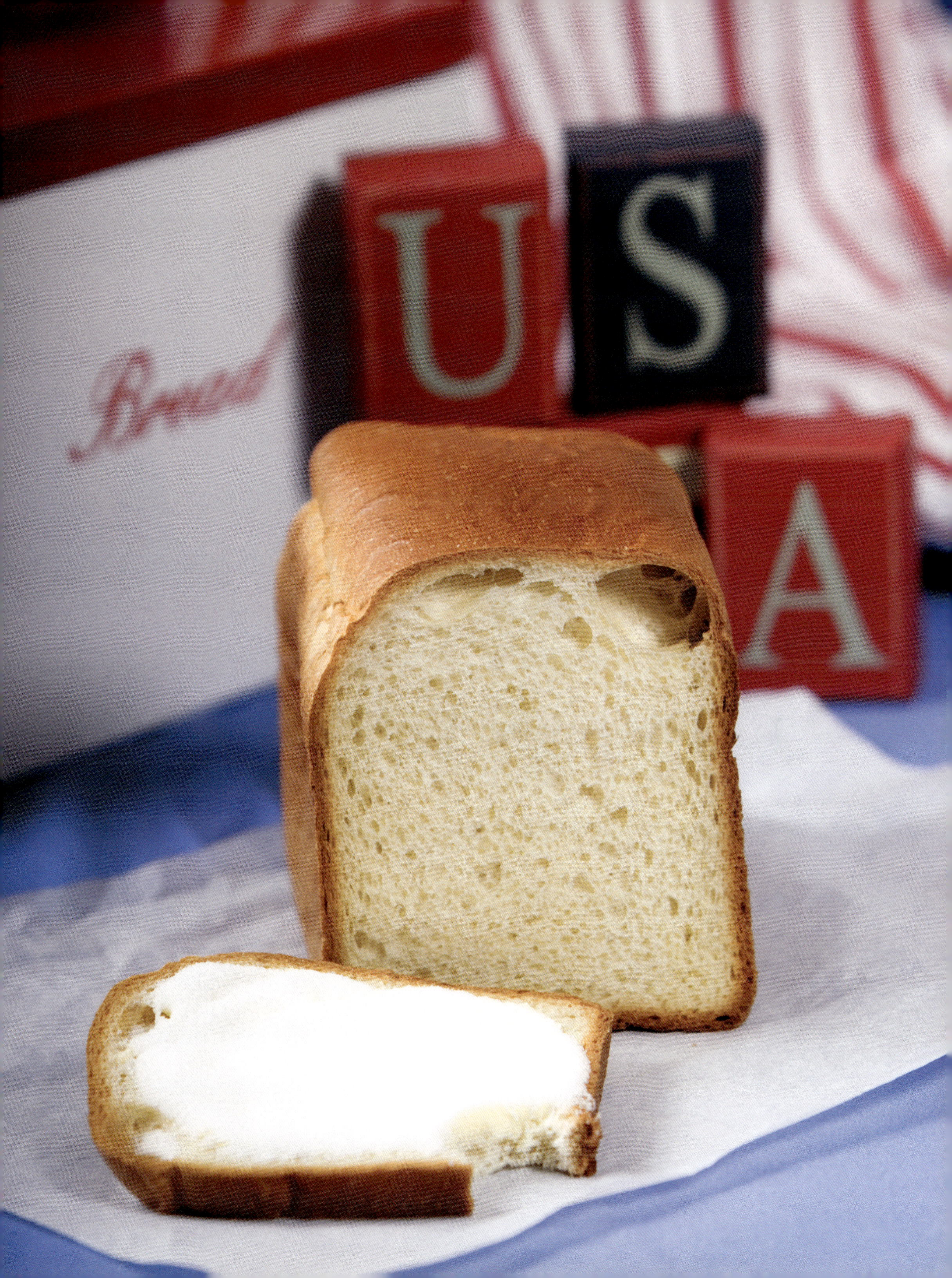
Bread
U
S
A

Challah

Makes 1 loaf

Ingredients

6 large eggs
3 tablespoons honey
⅓ cup vegetable oil
1 tablespoon kosher salt
1 teaspoon apple cider vinegar
3 cups unbleached all purpose flour
1 tablespoon bread machine yeast

Challah is a traditional Jewish braided bread served on the Sabbath. Due to the very high percentage of eggs this bread contains, it is a beautiful golden color both inside and out. This is very sticky dough that is perfectly suited for the bread machine. After the second rise in the cycle, I like to take the dough out and braid it, then return it to the bread maker for the final rise and bake. While this step is not necessary, but rather decorative, it gives me an excuse to touch the dough, which is something I really enjoy. If you do not braid it, lightly slit the top of the dough before the baking cycle starts to prevent a crack from forming along one side.

1. Place all ingredients in the order listed into the bread maker; close lid.

2. Press MENU and select BASIC.

3. Press SIZE and select LARGER.

4. Press COLOR and select DARK.

5. Press START.

6. Total machine time is 3 hours.

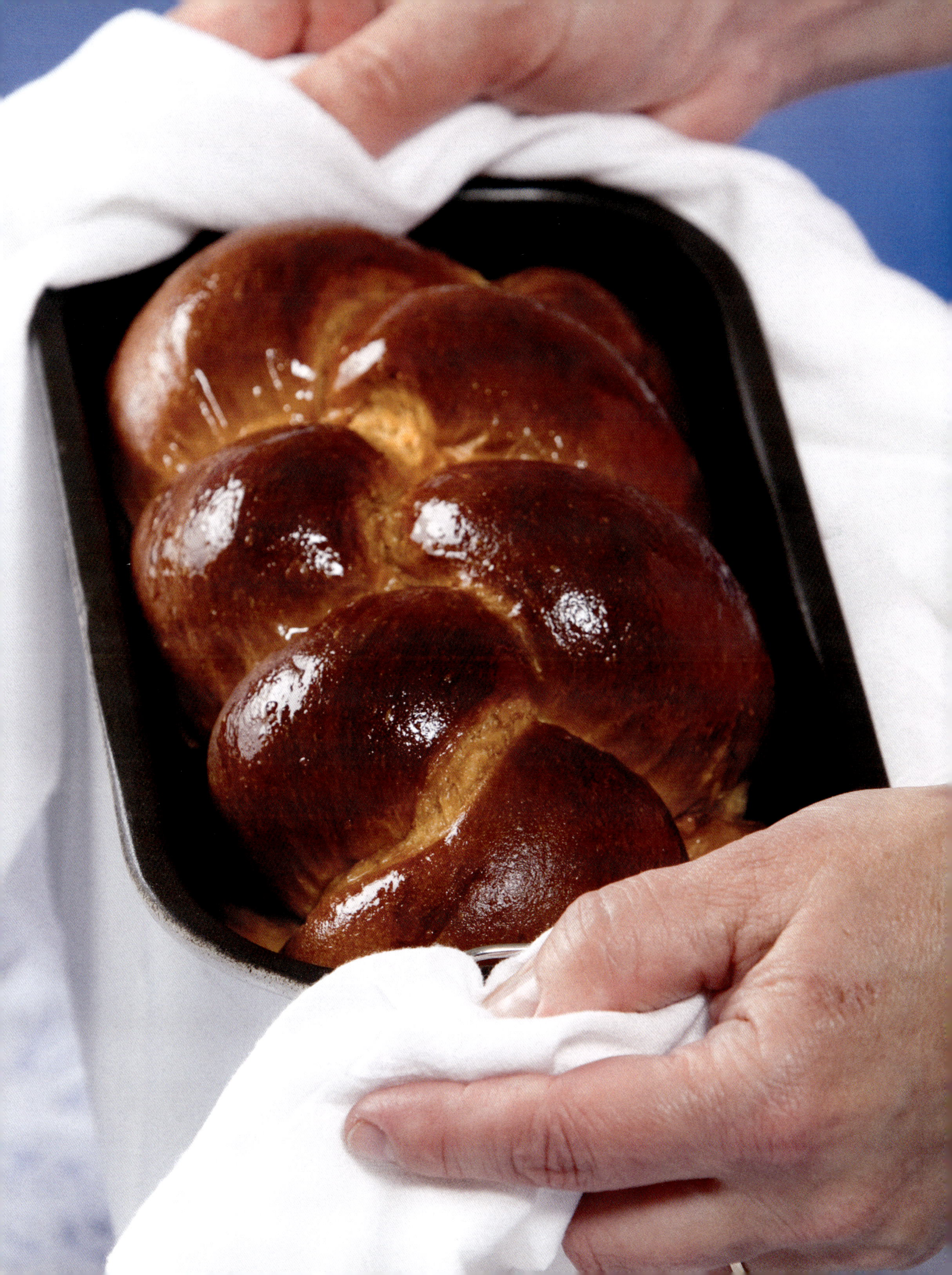

Pumpernickel Bread

Makes 1 loaf

Ingredients

1 cup water
4 tablespoons vegetable oil
2 tablespoons juice from a jar of dill pickles
3 tablespoons molasses
1 tablespoon vital wheat gluten
1 tablespoon caraway seed
2 tablespoons soy sauce

1 cup whole grain rye flour
½ cup 100% whole wheat flour
3 tablespoons cocoa powder
1½ cups unbleached bread flour
1½ teaspoons bread machine yeast
½ teaspoon diastatic malt powder (optional)
1 teaspoon kosher salt

Containing some interesting ingredients, like dill pickle juice and cocoa, this pumpernickel bread recipe (my brother John's favorite) will fill your home with a divine smell. Although some bakers make their pumpernickel without cocoa, I prefer to use it. The cocoa adds a hint of flavor and greatly contributes to the color. A slice of this untoasted bread, spread with cream cheese is simply heavenly for breakfast. I also recommend it as an open-faced, broiled pastrami sandwich. Put some Swiss cheese over the meat and broil it until melted and bubbly. Don't forget to served it with Russian dressing on the side. You can also serve this bread as an appetizer, sliced into thin triangles, spread with sour cream, and topped with smoked salmon and paper-thin slices of red onion.

1. Place all ingredients in the order listed into the bread maker; close lid.

2. Press MENU and select WHOLE WHEAT.

3. Press SIZE and select LARGER.

4. Press COLOR and select DARK.

5. Press START.

6. Total machine time is 3 hours and 40 minutes.

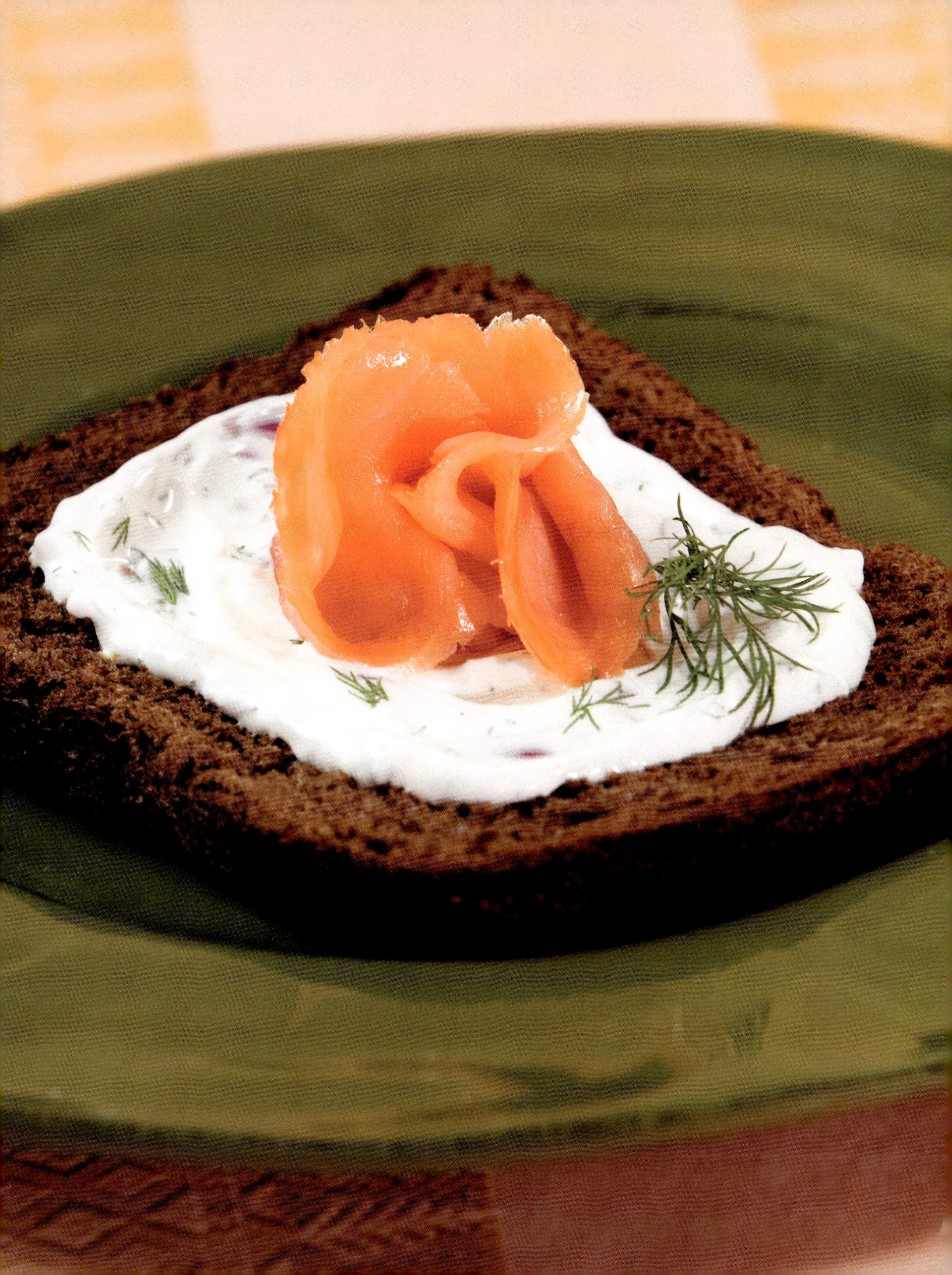

English Muffin Bread

Makes 1 loaf

Ingredients

1¼ cups water
2 tablespoons extra-virgin olive oil
1 tablespoon honey
1 tablespoon vital wheat gluten
½ teaspoon diastatic malt powder (optional)
1 tablespoon kosher salt
⅓ cup coarse cornmeal
3 cups unbleached bread flour
2 teaspoons bread machine yeast

This cornmeal recipe is another loaf that is very versatile and always welcome at my supper table. I make this recipe when I use my rice cooker or slow cooker to create a lazy, but delicious supper. Using the CUSTOM setting, I can program my bread maker to have a hot loaf of bread ready at the same time the rice cooker or slow cooker food is ready. Imagine coming home to a house filled with the smell of a heavenly pot roast and some homemade bread.

1. Place all ingredients in the order listed into the bread maker; close lid.
2. Press MENU and select BASIC.
3. Press SIZE and select LARGER.
4. Press COLOR and select MEDIUM.
5. Press START.
6. Total machine time is 3 hours.

Marian's Tip:
This bread makes wonderful grilled cheese sandwiches.

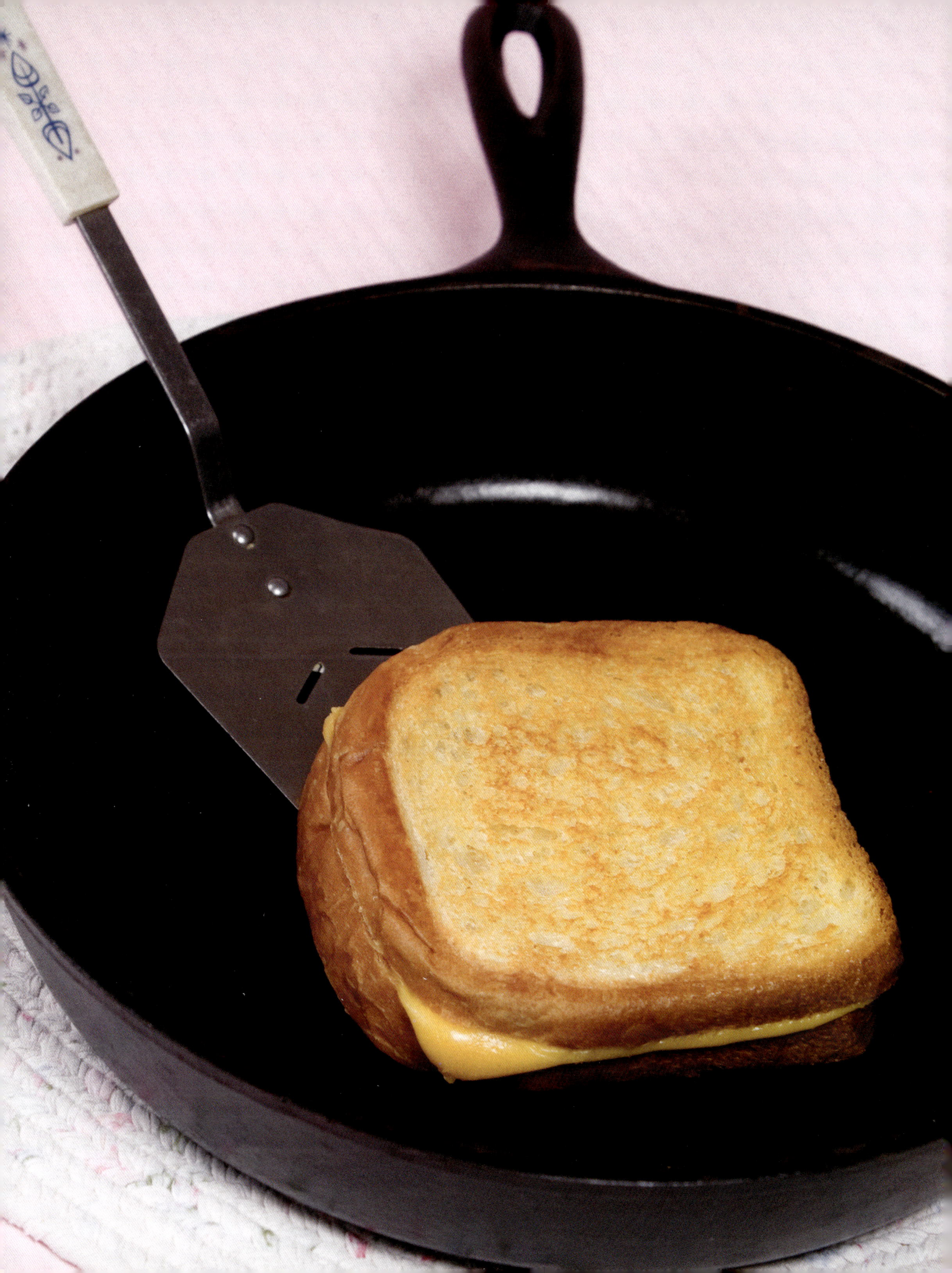

French Bread

Makes 1 loaf

Ingredients

1 cup + 1 tablespoon water
1 tablespoon kosher salt
3 cups unbleached bread flour
2 teaspoons bread machine yeast

This is one of the easiest breads to throw together with a short list of ingredients. This loaf will be a pale tan color when finished. Since the recipe contains no fat or sugar, this loaf tends to stick to the pan so let the bread cool for at least 20 minutes after baking. If I become too impatient to wait, I simply wrap the hot bread pan in a kitchen towel, set it down on the dining room table and tear off pieces to enjoy with dinner. The taste and crustiness of this bread is amazing.

1. Place all ingredients in the order listed into the bread maker; close lid.

2. Press MENU and select FRENCH.

3. Press SIZE and select LARGER.

4. Press COLOR and select DARK.

5. Press START.

6. Total machine time is 3 hours and 50 minutes.

Marian's Tip:
This bread tends to stick to the pan. To make it easier to remove, let it rest for 20 minutes after baking.

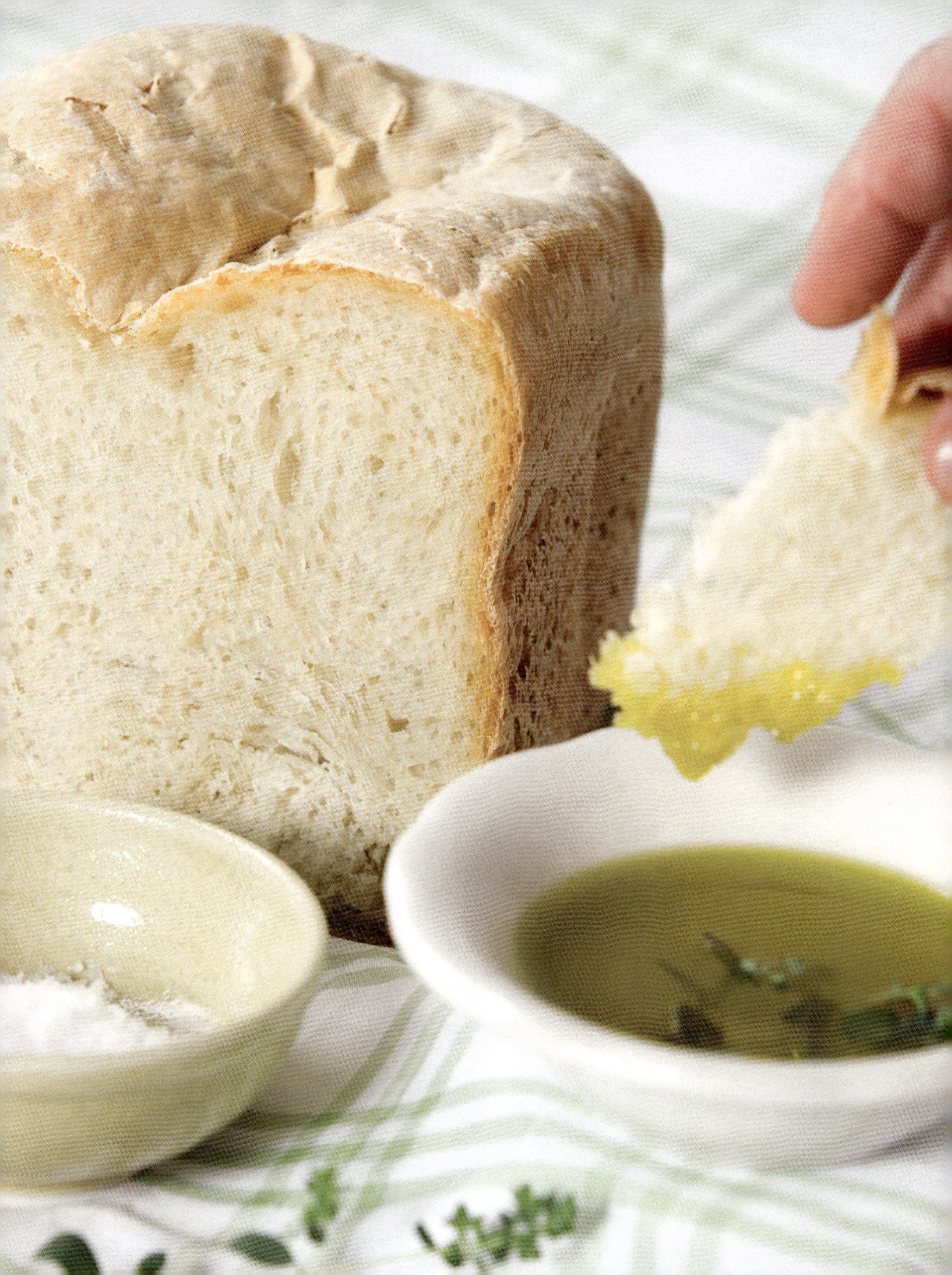

Chili Cheese Bread

Makes 1 loaf

Ingredients

½ cup water
1 can (4.5 ounces) green chiles
2 tablespoons tomato paste
¼ cup vegetable oil
1 tablespoon kosher salt
2 tablespoons chili powder
1 teaspoon onion powder
½ teaspoon red pepper flakes
⅓ cup queso fresco or Parmesan cheese, grated
3 cups unbleached bread flour
2½ teaspoons bread machine yeast

When my boys were little, I developed this bread as an American twist on a tortilla. I would make sandwiches using single slices of this bread, topped with mild pork carnitas or seasoned hamburgers, very finely shredded cabbage, chopped onions and lots of fresh cilantro. I would fold the bread in half, into what we called "Benders" or "Mortimers" and we would eat them like a taco. I don't know how they got those silly names, but they are really scrumptious and we still enjoy them to this day.

1. Place all ingredients in the order listed into the bread maker; close lid.

2. Press MENU and select BASIC.

3. Press SIZE and select LARGER.

4. Press COLOR and select MEDIUM.

5. Press START.

6. Total machine time is 3 hours.

Marian's Tip:
I like to turn any leftovers from this loaf into bread crumbs and sprinkle them over a chili cheese bake or enchilada casserole.

Easy Very Cheesy Bread

Makes 1 loaf

Ingredients

1 cup + 1 tablespoon water
3 tablespoons olive oil
1 tablespoon sugar
2 tablespoons powdered milk
1 tablespoon kosher salt
2 teaspoons vital wheat gluten

2/3 cup Parmesan cheese, grated
1/3 cup sharp cheddar cheese, cut into tiny cubes
1/3 cup Swiss cheese, cut into tiny cubes
3 cups unbleached bread flour
2 teaspoons bread machine yeast

This bread looks really interesting. Its crust is dark and a bit shaggy with nice, crusty bits of deeply toasted cheese. The interior is light, with dots of melted cheese. Smelling like a toasted cheese sandwich but only better, this bread tastes great all by itself or accompanied by a cup of soup. This is my mom's favorite bread and whenever she makes it, she substitutes the cheddar for her favorite cheese, Gouda. I also like to make the dough for this in the bread maker. I simply take it out, divide the bread into 3 long pieces, braid it and put it back into the pan to let it rise and bake. I do this just so it looks pretty. Regardless of how you make it, it is a beautiful and tall loaf that will make everyone happy.

1. Place all ingredients in the order listed into the bread maker; close lid.

2. Press MENU and select BASIC.

3. Press SIZE and select LARGER.

4. Press COLOR and select MEDIUM.

5. Press START.

6. Total machine time is 3 hours.

All-American Hamburger Buns

Makes 10 buns

Ingredients

1 cup + 1 tablespoon water
1 large egg
3 tablespoons powdered milk
2½ teaspoons bread machine yeast

2 tablespoons granulated sugar
2 tablespoons unsalted butter, softened
3 cups unbleached all purpose flour
1 tablespoon kosher salt

My family loves hamburgers. One day Jordan, my oldest son, suggested that while the meat and the filling part were always great, perhaps we needed to create a better bun. After many delicious test batches, we finally came up with this one. Here are the criteria we came up with for measuring a great bun:

- It has to be golden brown and soft enough to squash down a bit when you pick up the burger.
- It has to be tender enough so that when you take a bite, nothing comes out the other end.
- It needs to have a great wheat flavor that is faintly sweet.

If you love a good burger as much as my family does, I'm sure you will absolutely enjoy these buns.

1. Place all ingredients in the order listed into the bread maker; close lid.

2. Press MENU and select DOUGH.

3. Press START.

4. Total machine time is 1 hour and 30 minutes.

5. Remove dough and cut it into 10 equal pieces. Roll each piece under your palm until it forms a smooth ball.

6. Place balls, evenly spaced, on a greased or parchment-lined baking tray; allow balls to rise under a soft kitchen towel for 30 minutes.

7. Bake in the oven at 375 degrees for 15-20 minutes or until golden brown.

Marian's Tip:
For added texture and flavor, brush dough with beaten egg white and sprinkle with finely diced onions, sesame seeds or chopped fresh herbs before baking.

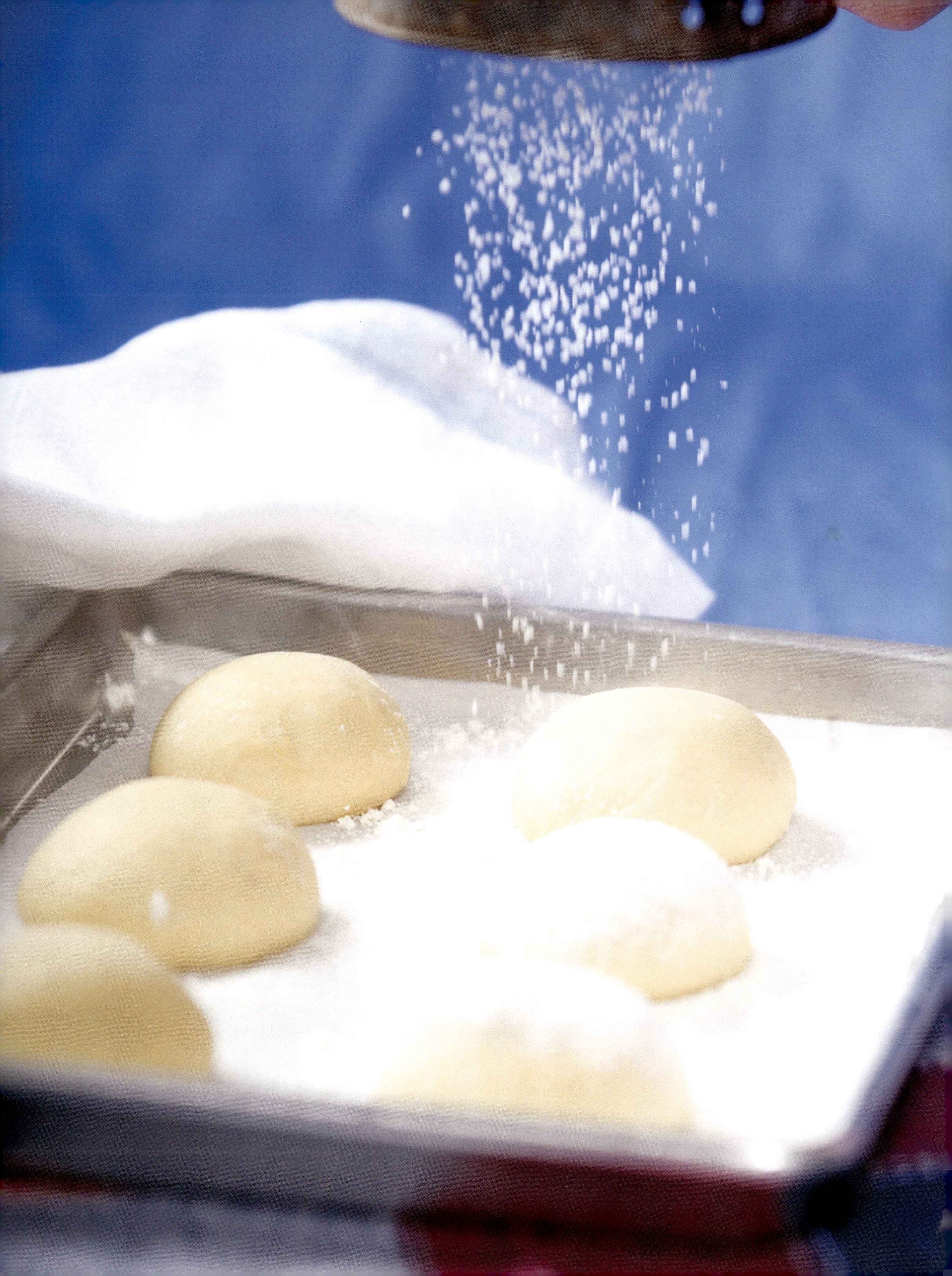

Kalamata Olive Sourdough Bread

Makes 1 loaf

Ingredients

1 cup water
⅓ cup sourdough starter (see recipe on page 43)
4 tablespoons extra-virgin olive oil
1 tablespoon honey
3 tablespoons powdered milk
1 tablespoon vital wheat gluten
1 tablespoon kosher salt
½ cup 100% whole wheat flour
2½ cups unbleached bread flour
2 teaspoons bread machine yeast
1 cup packed Kalamata olives, pitted

Perfect for a pasta meal, this loaf, giving you a big olive taste in every bite, is positively bursting with olives. I included some 100% whole-wheat flour to give the loaf its body and sturdy crumb. This loaf will rise just to the top of the pan and then crest a bit above it during baking. Remember that when you add heavy ingredients to bread dough, like olives, it makes them a bit shorter. I typically serve it in a bread basket. We just tear off some pieces, dip them into a little fruity olive oil and add a schmear of roasted garlic. Delicious!

1. Place all ingredients, except olives, into the bread maker; close lid.

2. Press MENU and select BASIC.

3. Press SIZE and select LARGER.

4. Press COLOR and select DARK.

5. Press START.

6. About 22 minutes into the cycle, bread maker will beep twice; add olives and close the lid.

7. Total machine time is 3 hours.

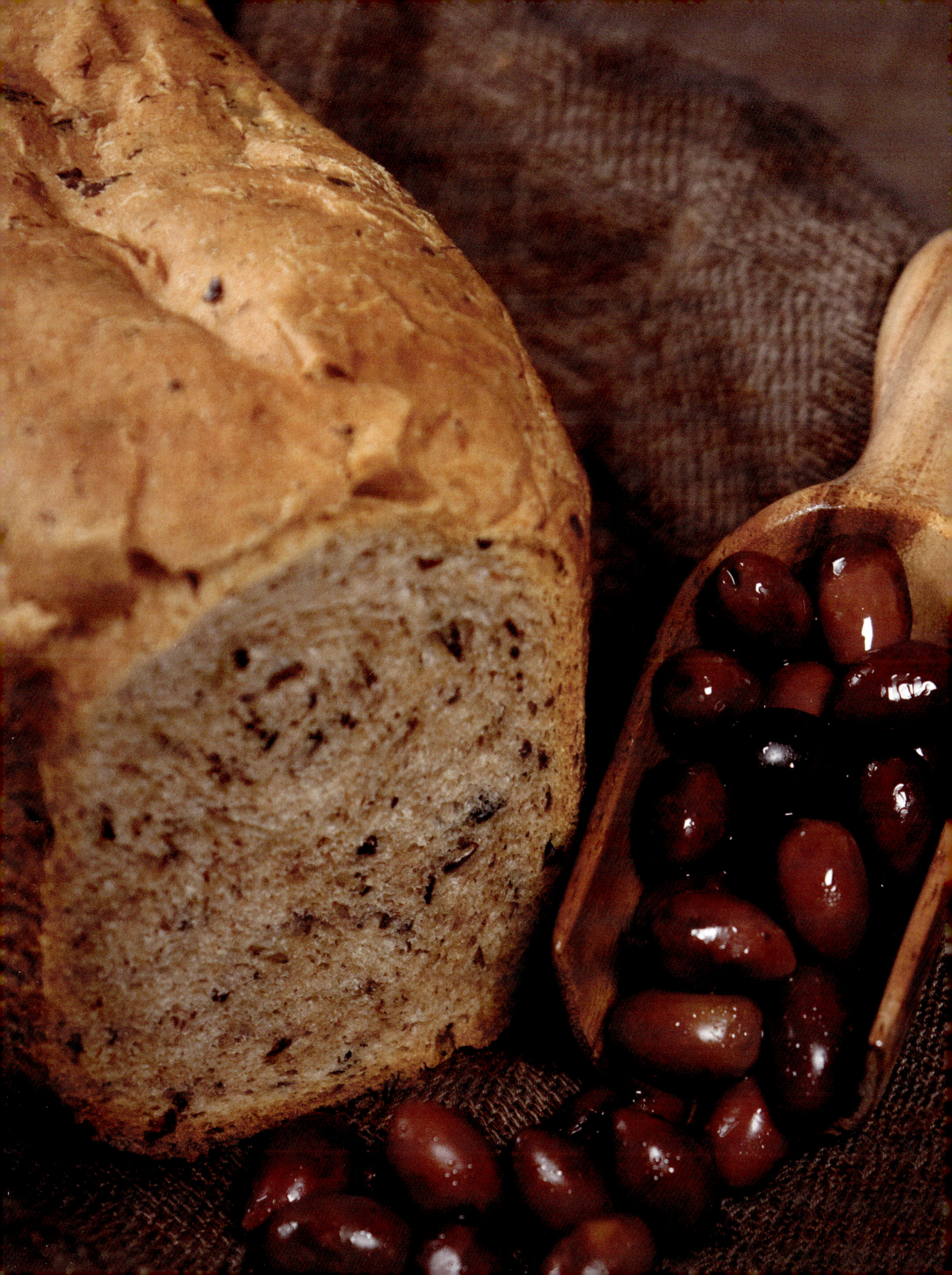

Kansas Sunflower Seed Bread

Makes 1 loaf

Ingredients

1 cup + 1 tablespoon water
5 tablespoons unsalted butter, softened
1 large egg
2 tablespoons sugar
3 tablespoons powdered milk
4 teaspoons vital wheat gluten
1 tablespoon kosher salt
3 cups unbleached bread flour
1 cup sunflower seeds, lightly toasted
2 teaspoons bread machine yeast

Ottawa is a charming town in Kansas with kind townspeople, lots of Victorian homes and a vast surrounding of farms with crops such as milo, wheat and sunflowers. It is the kind of town where family doctors still deliver medicine to your doorstep on their way home. I lived in this small town for twelve years. I went to a university there, met and married my husband Greg and had our two sons. A dear lady from the Baptist church gave me this delicious recipe. She simply called it "prairie bread" and I have adapted it for the bread machine. This loaf is flecked with nutty sunflower seeds and has a mild taste.

1. Place all ingredients in the order listed into the bread maker; close lid.
2. Press MENU and select BASIC.
3. Press SIZE and select LARGER.
4. Press COLOR and select MEDIUM.
5. Press START.
6. Total machine time is 3 hours.

Marian's Tip:
My favorite way to eat this bread is toasted, cut into fingers and dipped into the yolk of a soft boiled egg.

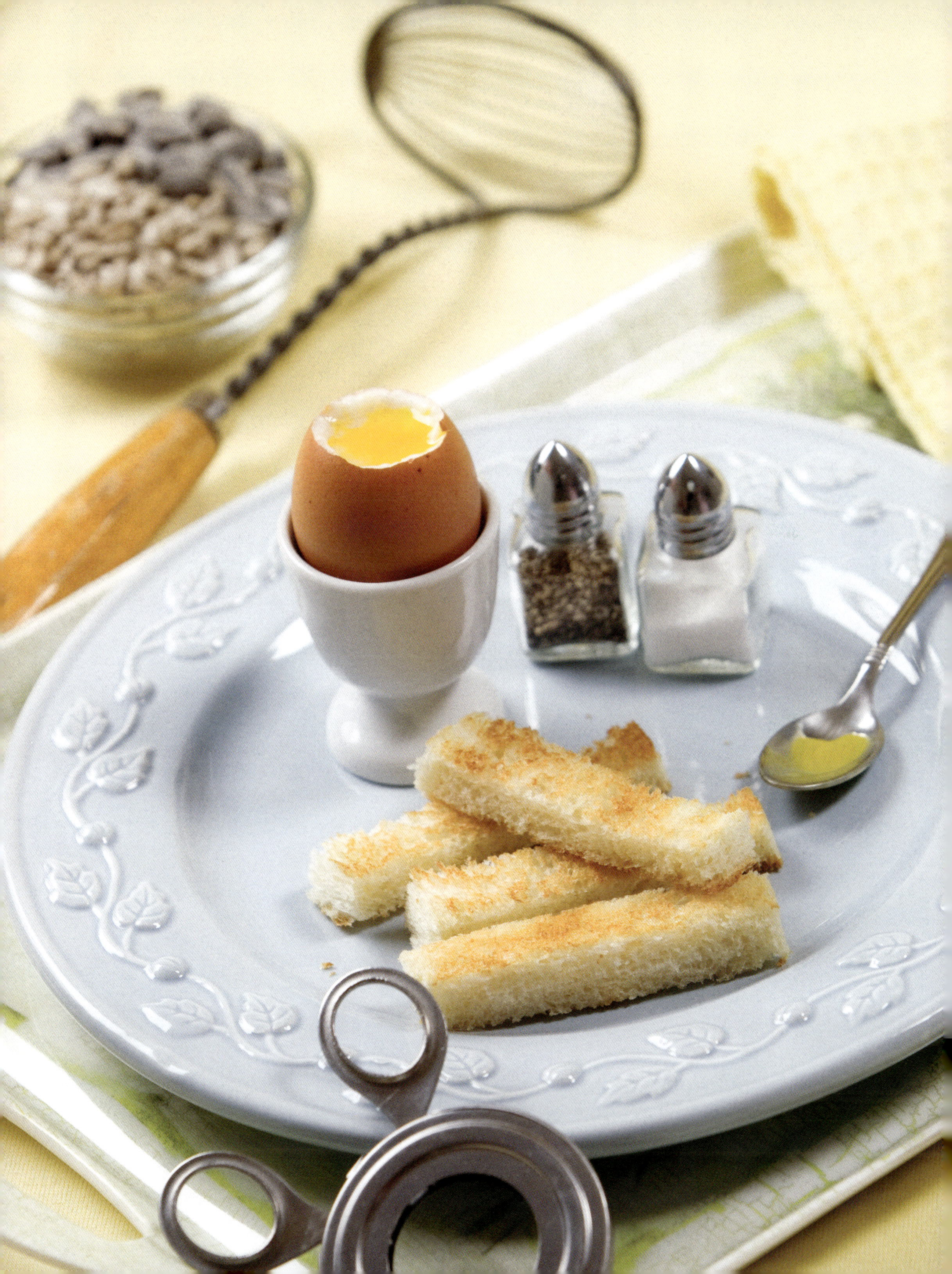

Focaccia Bread

Makes 1 loaf

Ingredients

1¼ cups water
4 tablespoons extra-virgin olive oil
1 tablespoon kosher salt
1 tablespoon honey
3 cups unbleached bread flour

1 tablespoon vital wheat gluten
12 sage leaves (optional)
½ cup walnuts (optional)
1 tablespoon bread machine yeast

While this is not a traditional looking focaccia, it is a very quick (59 minutes) recipe to make. I enjoy making this recipe when I am pressed for time but hungry for homemade bread. If you want to make it in the traditional shape, you can mix it in the bread maker, then remove the dough, pat it into a rough oval and place it on an oiled baking sheet. Dimple the dough all over using your fingertips then drizzle it with more extra-virgin olive oil and salt. Let the dough rest then bake it in the oven at 450 degrees for 20 minutes or until deeply browned. I love serving this with roasted garlic.

1. Place all ingredients in the order listed into the bread maker; close lid.

2. Press MENU and select RAPID BAKE.

3. Press COLOR and select DARK.

4. Press START.

5. Total machine time is 59 minutes.

Marian's Tip:
As a variation, substitute the sage and walnuts with 2 tablespoons chopped rosemary and ½ cup sun dried tomatoes or ½ cup chopped black olives as well as 2 tablespoons chopped thyme.

Onion & Sage White Bread

Makes 1 loaf

Ingredients

1 cup water
2 tablespoons olive oil
2 tablespoons fresh sage, roughly chopped
½ cup yellow onions, diced
1 tablespoon packed light brown sugar

4 tablespoons powdered milk
4 teaspoons vital wheat gluten
1 tablespoon kosher salt
3 cups unbleached bread flour
2 teaspoons bread machine yeast

Sage is my favorite herb. I love the combination of onion and sage and use it in many savory dishes I make. It is no surprise that I came up with a recipe for it in a loaf of bread as well. This bread makes excellent sandwiches. I like turkey with softened cream cheese instead of mayo, lettuce, tomato, and a bit of Russian dressing for sweetness. If you have any leftovers, cut it into cubes and sauté it in a bit of olive oil to make wonderful salad croutons.

1. Place all ingredients in the order listed into the bread maker; close lid.

2. Press MENU and select BASIC.

3. Press SIZE and select LARGER.

4. Press COLOR and select MEDIUM.

5. Press START.

6. Total machine time is 3 hours.

Sourdough Teff Bread

Makes 1 loaf

Ingredients

2/3 cup water
1 cup sourdough starter (see recipe on page 43)
5 tablespoons unsalted butter, softened
1 large egg
2 tablespoons honey
3 tablespoons powdered milk
4 teaspoons vital wheat gluten
1 tablespoon kosher salt
2½ cups unbleached bread flour
½ cup whole grain teff flour
1 teaspoon bread machine yeast

The sourdough starter is what gives this loaf a very special tang and aroma. Because the bread maker does the work in a relatively fast manner, you will still need to add a bit of yeast to the recipe. Teff, the tiniest grain grown and indigenous to Ethiopia and other parts of Africa, gives the loaf a dusky color and extra pleasant flavor. With its highly nutritious and elevated levels of lysine, the teff grain is worth seeking out and can be found in most health food stores.

1. Place all ingredients in the order listed into the bread maker; close lid.

2. Press MENU and select BASIC.

3. Press SIZE and select LARGER.

4. Press COLOR and select DARK.

5. Press START.

6. Total machine time is 3 hours.

Sourdough Starter

Makes 1 cup

Ingredients

½ cup unbleached all purpose flour
½ cup chlorine-free water
⅛ teaspoon bread machine yeast
2 tablespoons buttermilk

Why go to the trouble of making homemade sourdough starter? Because of the flavor! This recipe is a simple stir-together. After a few days, when the yeast is happily multiplying and bubbling away, simply remove a portion of it to add to any bread, muffin or pancake recipe. The flavor this type of starter adds to bread is incomparable and it is well worth the small effort to create. This starter can be kept in the refrigerator indefinitely.

1. In a 1-quart glass jar, combine all ingredients; stir until smooth.

2. Cover and let rest at room temperature for 3 days.

3. After 3 days, "feed" the starter with ½ cup flour and ½ cup water; cover and let rest at room temperature for 1 more day.

4. Starter is now ready to be used and should be kept in the refrigerator. To use, remove portion called for in the recipe.

Marian's Tip:
"Feed" the starter weekly, removing half of the starter each time before feeding. Some amber liquid will form on top of the starter. It is part of the natural fermentation process and should be stirred back into the starter. If starter turns color and spots appear, discard it.

French Bread with Sourdough Starter

Makes 1 loaf

Ingredients

1 cup + 2 tablespoons water
1/3 cup sourdough starter (see recipe on page 43)
1 tablespoon kosher salt
3 cups unbleached bread flour
1½ teaspoons bread machine yeast

While this loaf does not look like a traditional French baguette, it has all the taste and great crust of real French bread. Making your own sourdough starter is very easy and adds an amazing flavor that is worth the effort.

1. Place all ingredients in the order listed into the bread maker; close lid.

2. Press MENU and select FRENCH.

3. Press SIZE and select LARGER.

4. Press COLOR and select DARK.

5. Press START.

6. Total machine time is 3 hours and 50 minutes.

Marian's Tip:
This bread tends to stick to the pan. To make it easier to remove, let it rest for 20 minutes after baking.

Old Fashioned Rye Bread

Makes 1 loaf

Ingredients

1 cup water
¼ cup juice from a jar of dill pickles
2 tablespoons olive oil
1 tablespoon honey
3 teaspoons vital wheat gluten
1 tablespoon caraway seeds

2 teaspoons kosher salt
1 cup whole grain rye flour
½ cup 100% whole wheat flour
1½ cups unbleached bread flour
1½ teaspoons bread machine yeast

I received this recipe from a friend who was a pastry chef many years ago. I was immediately intrigued that the recipe called for the addition of pickle juice. It seems to add just the perfect flavor balance to this recipe. This makes an exceptionally handsome loaf, tall, with a dark crust and light interior.

1. Place all ingredients in the order listed into the bread maker; close lid.

2. Press MENU and select WHOLE WHEAT.

3. Press SIZE and select LARGER.

4. Press COLOR and select DARK.

5. Press START.

6. Total machine time is 3 hours and 40 minutes.

Savory Mushroom Bread

Makes 1 loaf

Ingredients

1 cup water
¼ teaspoon ground black pepper
1 garlic clove, chopped
¼ cup yellow onion, chopped
4 tablespoons brown butter (see recipe on page 57)
1 tablespoon kosher salt
1 tablespoon soy sauce
¼ cup Parmesan cheese
1 tablespoon vital wheat gluten
3 cups unbleached bread flour
2½ teaspoons bread machine yeast
2 cups dried mushrooms

We are the type of people who never had a dish that had too many mushrooms in it. One day, my husband Greg asked, "What about making a mushroom bread?" I started this recipe off by using fresh mushrooms, sautéed them and then added them to the other ingredients. The flavor was too faint. I then added dried mushrooms, which I re-hydrated in water. While the flavor was better, it was still missing a big punch of flavor. Then, Greg suggested adding the dry mushrooms to the recipe straight from the container. Since I had never seen a recipe where dried mushrooms were added without re-hydrating them, I was very skeptical; however, it worked! Not only did the mushroom flavor come through with a big punch, the mushroom pieces also stayed together much better. Because there is a high volume of mushrooms and Parmesan cheese in this recipe, the loaf will not be as tall as other breads.

1. Place all ingredients in the order listed into the bread maker; close lid.

2. Press MENU and select BASIC.

3. Press SIZE and select LARGER.

4. Press COLOR and select DARK.

5. Press START.

6. Total machine time is 3 hours.

Marian's Tip:
You can buy dried mushrooms for a reasonable price at big club stores.

Sour Cream & Chive Bread

Makes 1 loaf

Ingredients

1 cup sour cream
¼ cup chives, snipped
1 tablespoon minced dried onions
½ cup water
1 large egg
4 tablespoons powdered milk

1 tablespoon + 1 teaspoon kosher salt
1 tablespoon vital wheat gluten
2 tablespoons granulated sugar
3 cups unbleached bread flour
2 teaspoons bread machine yeast

My daughter-in-law, Lindsay, loves sour cream so I came up with this recipe for her. Lindsay had never made homemade bread before, but I knew that if the recipe contained sour cream, she would probably make it. Sour cream is very special in the world of baking. It makes dough that is very silky and a joy to work with because it is far less sticky than dough that does not contain it. If you prefer, omit the dried onions as well as the chives and you have an exceptionally soft and delicious loaf, more similar to Buttercrust Bread.

1. Place all ingredients in the order listed into the bread maker; close lid.
2. Press MENU and select BASIC.
3. Press SIZE and select LARGER.
4. Press COLOR and select MEDIUM.
5. Press START.
6. Total machine time is 3 hours.

Confetti Veggie Bread

Makes 1 loaf

Ingredients

1 cup water
3 tablespoons olive oil
1 large egg
1 tablespoon honey
3 tablespoons powdered milk
2 teaspoons vital wheat gluten
1 tablespoon kosher salt

3½ cups bread flour
2 teaspoons bread machine yeast
¼ cup red bell pepper, diced
¼ cup green bell pepper, diced
¼ cup carrots, peeled and diced
¼ cup yellow onions, peeled and diced

This stunning loaf is tall and beautifully flecked with colorful pieces of peppers, onions and carrots. You can substitute other vegetables and add herbs. This bread makes the prettiest sandwiches, perfect for a picnic or to take to work to impress your coworkers.

1. Place all ingredients in the order listed into the bread maker; close lid.

2. Press MENU and select BASIC.

3. Press SIZE and select LARGER.

4. Press COLOR and select DARK.

5. Press START.

6. Total machine time is 3 hours.

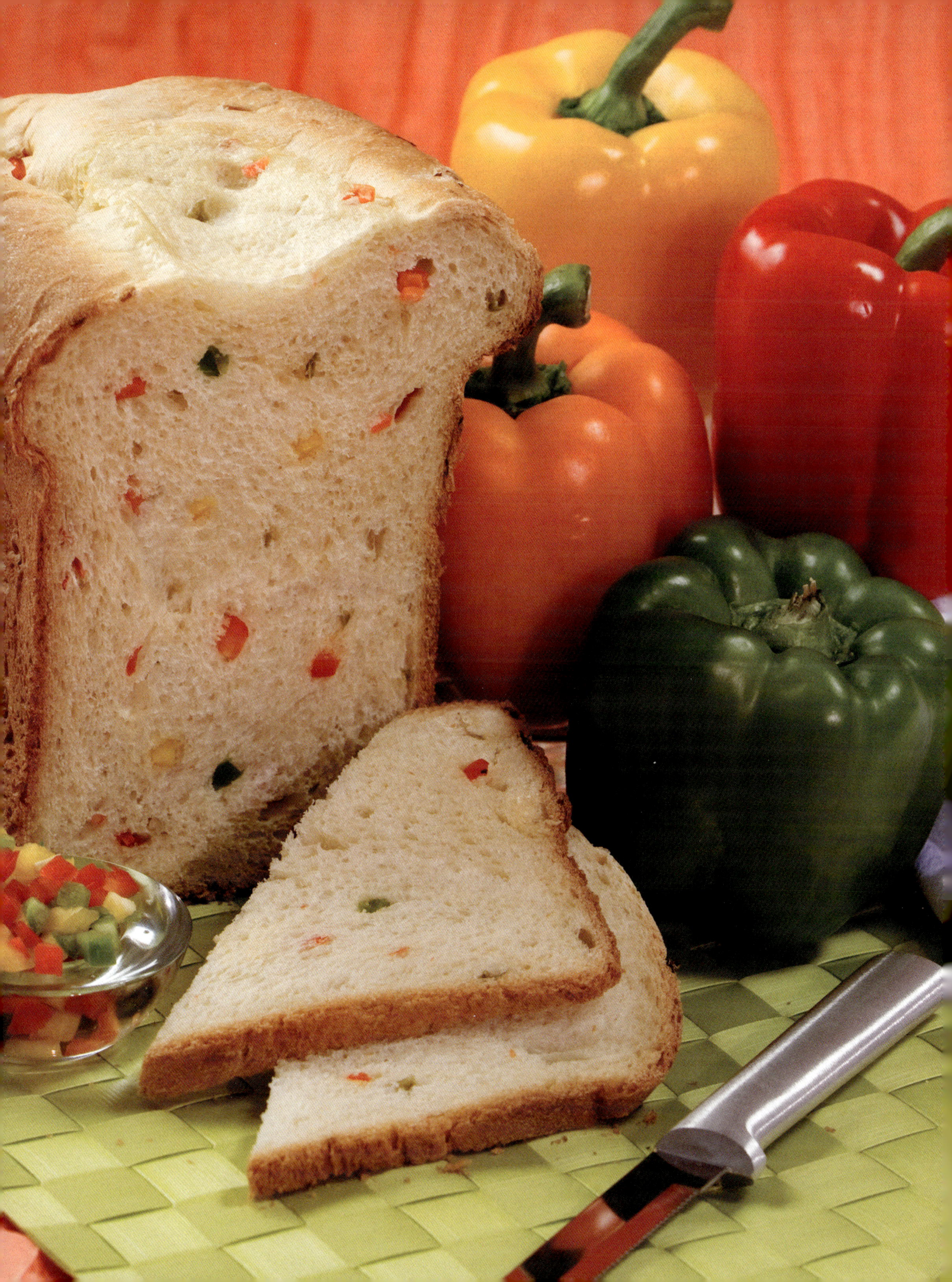

Pepperoni Pizza Bread

Makes 1 loaf

Ingredients

1¼ cups water
2 tablespoons extra-virgin olive oil
2 teaspoons granulated sugar
1 tablespoon kosher salt
4 teaspoons vital wheat gluten
½ cup Parmesan cheese, grated
¼ cup mozzarella cheese, shredded

1 package (3½ ounces) pepperoni, sliced
2 tablespoons tomato paste
1 garlic clove, minced
2 teaspoons dry Italian seasoning
3 cups unbleached bread flour
2½ teaspoons bread machine yeast
½ teaspoon additional kosher salt

My husband Greg was in the pizza business for many years. It just came naturally that I would come up with a pizza-flavored loaf of bread. If you love pizza as much as I do, this is the right bread for you. Your taste buds are in for a treat!

1. Place all ingredients, except the last measure of salt, in the order listed into the bread maker; close lid.

2. Press MENU and select BASIC.

3. Press SIZE and select LARGER.

4. Press COLOR and select MEDIUM.

5. Press START.

6. Set a kitchen timer for 1 hour and 40 minutes.

7. When timer rings, lift lid and sprinkle the remaining ½ teaspoon of salt evenly over the top of the bread; close lid.

8. Total machine time is 2 hours and 50 minutes.

Wolf's Pizza Dough

Makes 2 pizzas

Ingredients

1 cup water
2 tablespoons olive oil
1 tablespoon honey

1 teaspoon kosher salt
3 cups unbleached bread flour
2½ teaspoons bread machine yeast

This is the pizza dough recipe that is used at all of Wolf's restaurants. It is not only the best I have ever tasted, but it is a pleasure to work with. I remember when I was the pastry chef at Wolf's café in Orlando; he was there for a wine dinner to raise money for one of his favorite charities, Meals-On-Wheels. I was helping to stretch out all of the pizza dough needed for his signature Smoked Salmon Pizza that we would be serving that night. I was new to stretching pizza dough, and when Wolf saw my attempts (flat, lipless, misshapen pizza dough), he laughed and asked, "Making tortillas or pizzas, Madame?" Although I was embarrassed, I have always enjoyed his humor. He then proceeded to give me an excellent, one-on-one lesson on how to make beautiful pizzas. Lessons like that are priceless.

1. Place all ingredients in the order listed into the bread maker; close lid.

2. Press MENU and select DOUGH.

3. Press START.

4. Total machine time is 1 hour and 30 minutes.

5. When cycle is complete, divide dough into two dough balls.

6. To make a pizza, stretch the dough until desired thickness, add your favorite toppings and bake in the oven at 500 degrees for 12-15 minutes or until crust is a rich brown color.

Marian's Tip:
To freeze raw dough balls, spray the inside of a zipper bag with non-stick cooking spray before adding the dough balls. Freeze for up to 2 months. Thaw before use.

Wild Rice Bread

Makes 1 loaf

Ingredients

1 cup water
2 tablespoons molasses
1 tablespoon soy sauce
3 tablespoons brown butter (see recipe on page 57)
1 large egg
1 teaspoon diastatic malt powder
3 tablespoons powdered milk

2 teaspoons vital wheat gluten
2 teaspoons lecithin (optional)
1 tablespoon kosher salt
1½ cups cooked wild rice
3½ cups unbleached bread flour
2 teaspoons bread machine yeast

Wild rice is terrific in a loaf of bread because the chewy grains keep the bread nice and moist. The state of Minnesota grows most of our nation's wild rice, which is not really rice at all, but grass. The molasses and soy sauce add a real depth of flavor and both of these ingredients are common in whole-grain breads. The soy helps to counteract the "bird seedy" nature that heavier whole-grain loaves tend to have. Not only does brown butter add even more flavor, but it is also one of my favorite ingredients. I add lecithin (made from soybeans) to improves the shelf life of this bread as it contains more costly ingredients.

1. Place all ingredients in the order listed into the bread maker; close lid.

2. Press MENU and select BASIC.

3. Press SIZE and select LARGER.

4. Press COLOR and select DARK.

5. Press START.

6. Total machine time is 3 hours.

Marian's Tip:
I always use my rice cooker when cooking any type of rice, even wild rice. The texture of the rice is perfect every time.

Thanksgiving Bread

Makes 1 loaf

Ingredients

1 cup water
2 tablespoons unsalted butter, softened
1 tablespoon packed light brown sugar
1 teaspoon balsamic vinegar
4 tablespoons powdered milk
4 teaspoons vital wheat gluten
1 tablespoon kosher salt
3 cups unbleached bread flour
2½ teaspoons bread machine yeast
3 tablespoons fresh sage, coarsely chopped
⅓ cup onion, chopped
¼ cup celery, chopped

Thanksgiving is my favorite holiday because it is all about family and food. I love the roasted turkey, stuffing, cranberry sauce and sweet potato casserole. I came up with this recipe because I not only love turkey sandwiches, but this bread tastes and smells just like Thanksgiving stuffing. I love mine with cranberry sauce on it. This recipe produces a very tall, handsome loaf that will fill your kitchen with the wonderful smell of Thanksgiving.

1. Place all ingredients in the order listed into the bread maker; close lid.
2. Press MENU and select BASIC.
3. Press SIZE and select LARGER.
4. Press COLOR and select DARK.
5. Press START.
6. Total machine time is 3 hours.

Whole Grain Oatmeal Bread

Makes 1 loaf

Ingredients

1 cup + 1 tablespoon water
2 tablespoons olive oil
1 tablespoon honey
1 large egg
½ cup whole grain rolled oats

3 tablespoons powdered milk
1 tablespoon vital wheat gluten
1 tablespoon kosher salt
3 cups unbleached bread flour
2½ teaspoons bread machine yeast

My Uncle Dave is a complete "foodie" and has been one of my main inspirations when it comes to cooking. Far away from any culinary literature, I spent the first eighteen years of my life in Congo, Africa. Being one of the most thoughtful gentlemen I have ever met, Uncle Dave would mail me cookbooks from America to Africa for my birthday each year. Without access to TV, electricity, libraries or the outside world, those precious cookbooks kept me inspired throughout my early years. This delicious bread is adapted from a recipe in one of the cookbooks Uncle Dave sent me in the early 1970's, and it has been a favorite of mine ever since.

1. Place all ingredients in the order listed into the bread maker; close lid.

2. Press MENU and select BASIC.

3. Press SIZE and select LARGER.

4. Press COLOR and select DARK.

5. Press START.

6. Total machine time is 3 hours.

Marian's Tip:
I like to brush the top of the loaf with a little water and sprinkle 1 tablespoon of whole grain rolled oats over the loaf just before the machine starts baking (about 1 hour and 45 minutes into the cycle).

Sweet Potato Bread

Makes 1 loaf

Ingredients

1½ cups sweet potatoes, cut into 1-inch cubes
1 cup water
2 tablespoons unsalted butter, softened
3 tablespoons packed light brown sugar
3 cups unbleached bread flour

1 tablespoon kosher salt
4 teaspoons vital wheat gluten
4 tablespoons powdered milk
2½ teaspoons bread machine yeast
1 large egg

This beautiful loaf is the result of my love for sweet potatoes. I love baked sweet potatoes and I even eat the cold leftovers, skin and all, for a late night snack. The color of this loaf is light orange with lovely squares of soft sweet potato peeking out. The taste is mild, slightly sweet and earthy with a moist, fine crumb. I also like to make this recipe using the DOUGH setting. I remove the dough, shape it into dinner rolls, let them rise and bake them in my conventional oven at 350 degrees for 15-20 minutes. This loaf also freezes well.

1. Microwave the sweet potatoes until tender.

2. Place remaining ingredients, except sweet potatoes, into the bread maker; close lid.

3. Press MENU and select SWEET.

4. Press SIZE and select LARGER.

5. Press COLOR and select DARK.

6. Press START.

7. About 20 minutes into the cycle, bread maker will beep twice; add sweet potatoes and close the lid.

8. Total machine time is 2 hours and 50 minutes.

Brown Butter Sandwich Bread

Makes 1 loaf

Ingredients

1 cup + 1 tablespoon water
5 tablespoons brown butter (see recipe on page 57)
1 large egg
2 tablespoons granulated sugar
3 tablespoons powdered milk
4 teaspoons vital wheat gluten
1 tablespoon kosher salt
3 cups unbleached bread flour
2 teaspoons bread machine yeast

The recipe for this bread came about from my love of brown butter. Brown butter is the secret flavor ingredient in many of my recipes. When butter is cooked, it takes on a totally different flavor and becomes caramely and very nutty. This loaf is perfect for sandwiches as well as toast. I love to turn the stale leftovers into a caramel pecan bread pudding. Making the brown butter is a quick process but you have to pay attention as it burns easily.

1. Place all ingredients in the order listed into the bread maker; close lid.

2. Press MENU and select BASIC.

3. Press SIZE and select LARGER.

4. Press COLOR and select DARK.

5. Press START.

6. Total machine time is 3 hours.

Brown Butter

Makes about 1 cup

Ingredients

1½ cups (3 sticks) unsalted butter

Brown butter is one of the great kitchen secrets and I always have a jar of it in my refrigerator. It is complex in flavor with a deep, caramelized and nutty aroma. Once you try this in place of regular butter, you will find many uses for it. My favorite pasta dish, at Wolf's café in Orlando, is the butternut squash ravioli. The sauce for that dish is a simple mix of a bit of brown butter, balsamic vinegar, pine nuts and sage.

1. In a sauté pan over medium heat, bring butter to a simmer; let cook until butter smells delightfully nutty and the color turns to a medium amber with small flecks of darker brown in the bottom of the pan.

2. Remove from heat immediately and pour into a wide heat-proof bowl to stop the cooking process.

3. Let cool to room temperature.

Marian's Tip:
Store refrigerated in an airtight container for up to 3 months.

Pistachio Nut Bread

Makes 1 loaf

Ingredients

1 cup water
2 tablespoons honey
1 large egg
5 tablespoons unsalted butter, softened
1 tablespoon kosher salt

3 tablespoons powdered milk
4 teaspoons vital wheat gluten
3 cups unbleached bread flour
2½ teaspoons bread machine yeast
1½ cups pistachio nuts, lightly toasted

Pistachio nuts are always a welcomed ingredient in baking because of their vibrant green color. In this loaf, they add their subtle charm and flavor in the form of tiny green delicious pockets speckled throughout the loaf. My preferred way to eat this bread is sliced, topped with a thin layer of butter and a sprinkle of kosher salt. It is utterly delicious.

1. Place all ingredients in the order listed into the bread maker; close lid.

2. Press MENU and select BASIC.

3. Press SIZE and select LARGER.

4. Press COLOR and select MEDIUM.

5. Press START.

6. Total machine time is 3 hours.

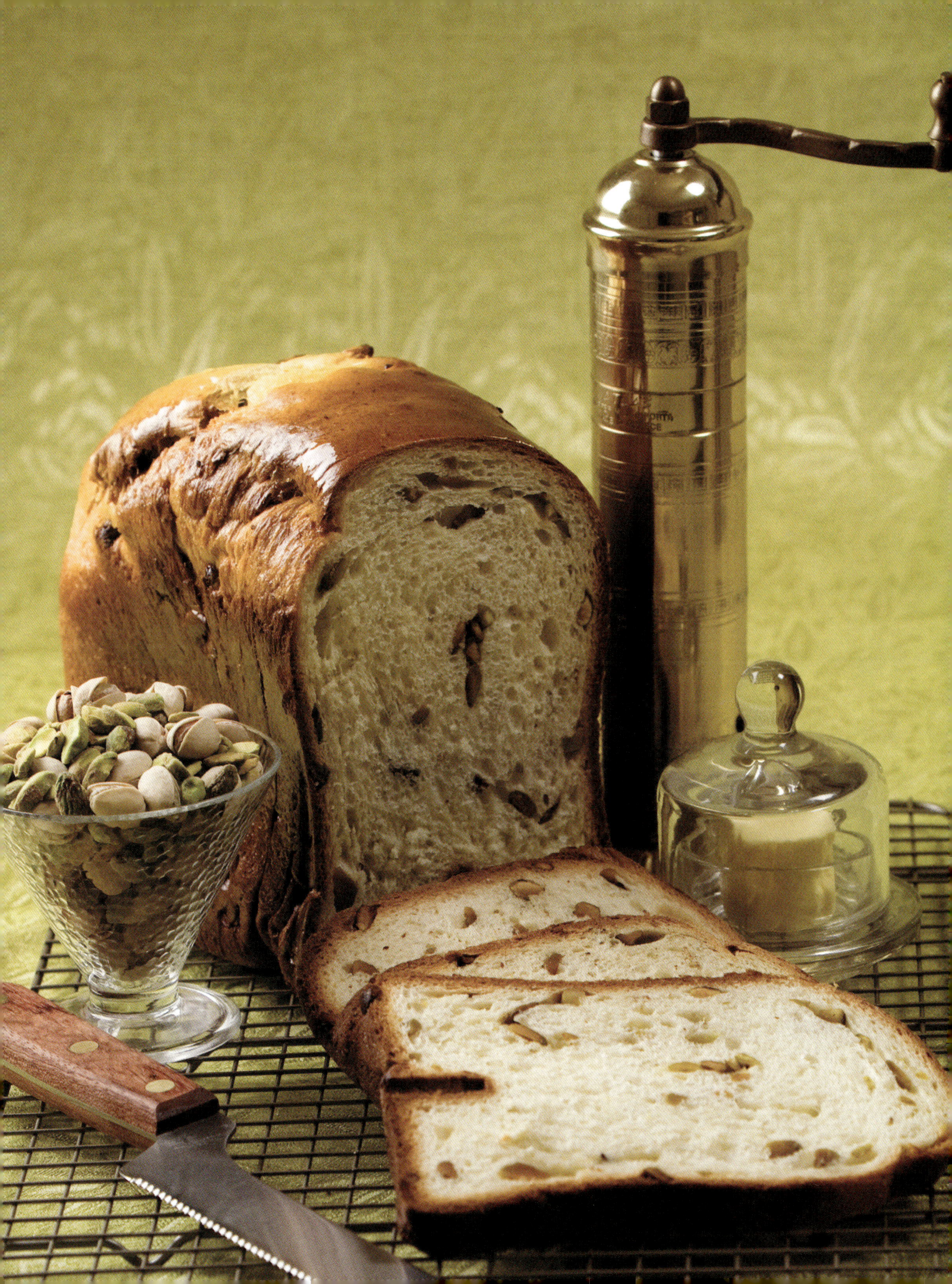

Cinnamon Raisin Bread

Makes 1 loaf

Ingredients

1 cup water
3 tablespoons unsalted butter, softened
1 teaspoon vanilla extract
1 large egg
1 teaspoon kosher salt
2 tablespoons ground cinnamon
3 tablespoons powdered milk
1 teaspoon diastatic malt powder (optional)
2 teaspoons vital wheat gluten
¼ cup granulated sugar
⅛ teaspoon citric acid
3 cups unbleached bread flour
2½ teaspoons bread machine yeast
½ cup raisins
½ cup pecan pieces, toasted

Just the smell of cinnamon raisin bread baking makes me smile. If you can find Vietnamese cinnamon for this recipe, you will like it even more. Vietnamese cinnamon is very aromatic and warm, with a sweeter taste than traditional cinnamon. This is a moist, dark loaf with a chewy crumb that is irresistible with a little schmear of cream cheese. Use any leftovers to make delicious French toast.

1. Place all ingredients, except raisins and pecans, in the order listed into the bread maker; close lid.

2. Press MENU and select SWEET.

3. Press SIZE and select LARGER.

4. Press COLOR and select DARK.

5. Press START.

6. About 22 minutes into the cycle, bread maker will beep twice; add raisins and pecans; close the lid.

7. Total machine time is 2 hours and 50 minutes.

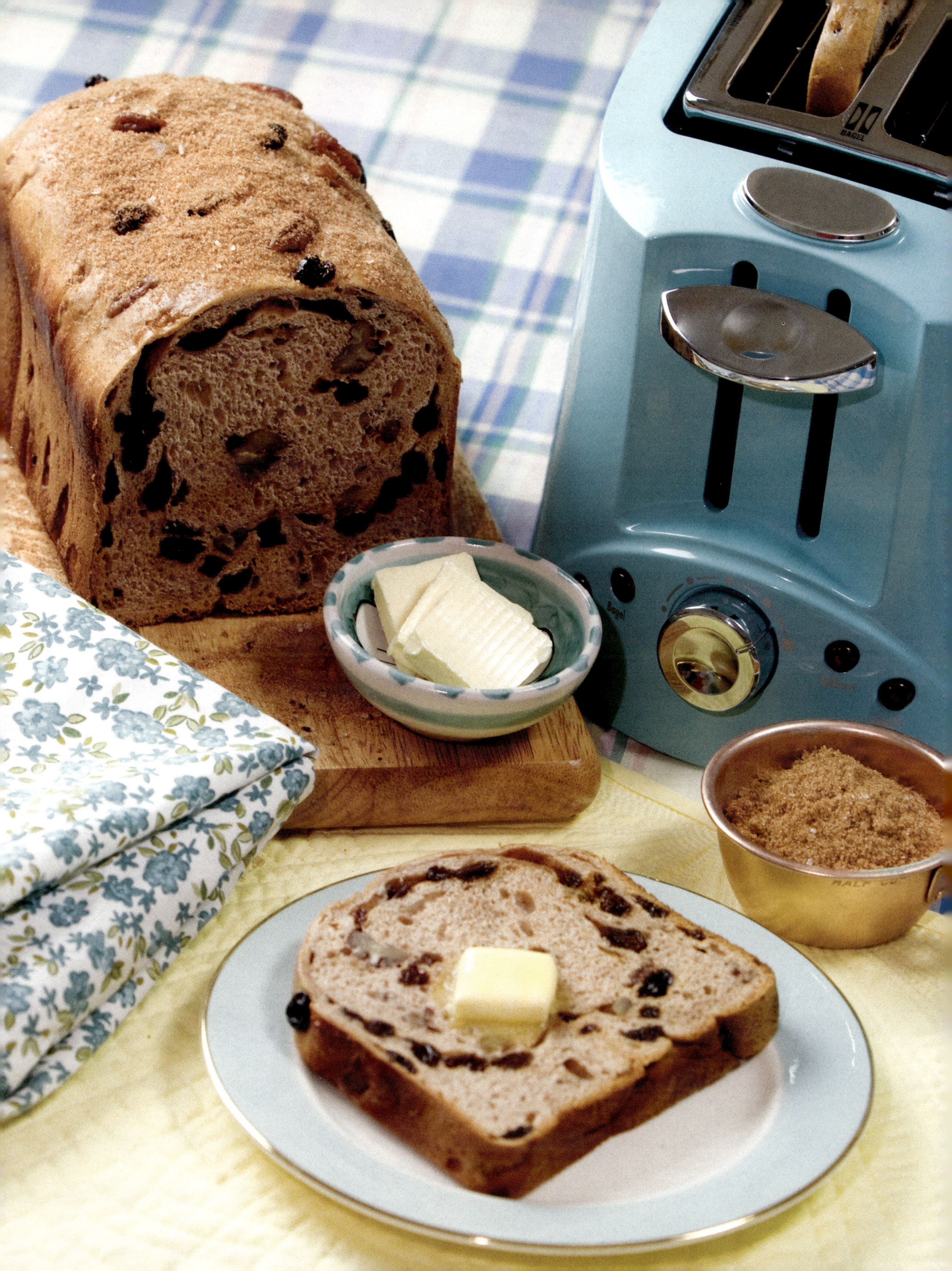
BAGEL

Coconut Yeast Bread

Makes 1 loaf

Ingredients

1 cup + 1 tablespoon water
1 large egg
5 tablespoons coconut oil
1 teaspoon pure coconut extract
2 tablespoons granulated sugar
1 cup sweetened coconut flakes
3 tablespoons powdered milk
1 tablespoon vital wheat gluten
1 tablespoon kosher salt
3 cups unbleached bread flour
1 tablespoon bread machine yeast

If you are a fan of Hawaiian or Portuguese sweet bread, you will love this loaf. It is coco nutty but not too sweet. Back in Africa, we had an abundance of coconut palms, so we used coconut quite often in our recipes. I remember using a sharp wooden stake that was driven into the ground to remove the fibrous husk of the coconut. Then, using the dull side of a machete, I would crack open the coconut and pry out the white flesh from the shell using a butter knife. Even though it was a lot of work, I always enjoyed it. This is the recipe we used to make whenever we wanted a change from plain white bread.

1. Place all ingredients in the order listed into the bread maker; close lid.

2. Press MENU and select BASIC.

3. Press SIZE and select LARGER.

4. Press COLOR and select DARK.

5. Press START.

6. Total machine time is 3 hours.

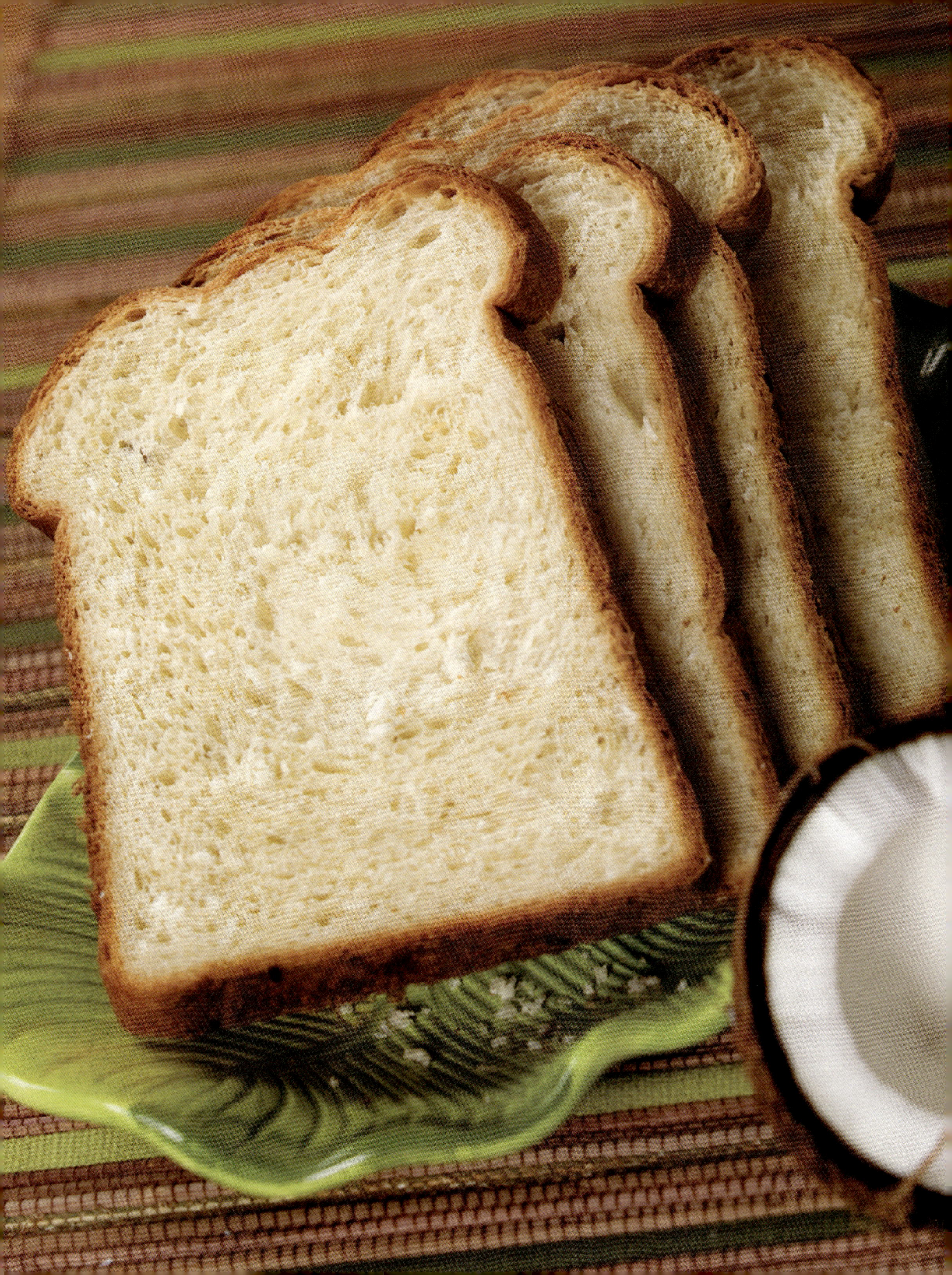

Hawaiian Sweet Bread

Makes 1 loaf

Ingredients

1 cup water
1 teaspoon pure vanilla extract
2 drops pure orange oil
2 drops pure lemon oil
2 large eggs
4 tablespoons unsalted butter, softened

¼ cup powdered milk
1 tablespoon kosher salt
6 tablespoons granulated sugar
3½ cups unbleached bread flour
2¼ teaspoons bread machine yeast

This bread is similar to brioche, but more feathery in texture. It is slightly sweet, delightfully squishy, with the faintest hint of citrus. Most Hawaiian bread recipes are derived from the Portuguese who settled on the islands long ago. My family loves this bread any way I serve it:
- plain, toasted with jam and butter.
- warm, in a bread basket with dinner.
- buttered and thickly sprinkled with sugar as a snack with a glass of milk.

1. Place all ingredients in the order listed into the bread maker; close lid.
2. Press MENU and select SWEET.
3. Press SIZE and select LARGER.
4. Press COLOR and select DARK.
5. Press START.
6. Total machine time is 2 hours and 50 minutes.

Marian's Tip:
If you don't have pure orange or lemon oil, you can use a ¼ teaspoon of orange or lemon zest instead.

Chocolaty Yeast Bread

Makes 1 loaf

Ingredients

1 cup water
5 tablespoons unsalted butter, softened
¼ cup granulated sugar
2 large eggs
2 teaspoons vanilla extract
1 teaspoon butter vanilla extract
4 tablespoons powdered milk

1 tablespoon vital wheat gluten
2 teaspoons kosher salt
⅓ cup good quality cocoa powder
3 cups + 2 tablespoons unbleached bread flour
2 teaspoons bread machine yeast
½ cup semi sweet chocolate chips

My answer to those sneaky chocolate cravings is this delicious, chocolaty yeast bread. I suggest trying a slice of this bread with a thick spread of my Cherry Jam (the recipe is on page 140). I also love using it to make peanut butter and sliced banana sandwiches. It is also great with mascarpone cheese and fresh strawberries. If you want a perfectly shaped loaf, cut a shallow slit in the top of the loaf just before the baking cycle begins to prevent a crack from forming during baking. This step is optional.

1. Place all ingredients, except chocolate chips, in the order listed into the bread maker; close lid.

2. Press MENU and select SWEET.

3. Press SIZE and select LARGER.

4. Press COLOR and select MEDIUM.

5. Press START.

6. About 22 minutes into the cycle, bread maker will beep twice; add chocolate chips and close the lid.

7. Total machine time is 2 hours and 50 minutes.

Quick Breads

Extra Corny Corn Bread	67
Poppyseed Bread	68
Mama Claire's Spoon Bread	69
Zucchini Bread	70
My Favorite Banana Bread	72
Blueberry Lemon Quick Bread	74
Cranberry Orange Quick Bread	76
Sour Cream Coffee Cake	78
Pumpkin Bread	80
Gingerbread Cake	81
Jordan & Ben's Brownies	82
Apple Sauce Quick Bread	84

Extra Corny Corn Bread

Makes 1 loaf

Ingredients

½ cup unsalted butter, softened
3 large eggs
⅓ cup granulated sugar
½ cup plain yogurt, preferably Greek
1 cup corn, fresh, frozen or canned
1 tablespoon baking powder
2 teaspoons kosher salt
½ cup corn meal
1½ cups unbleached all purpose flour

I married into a decidedly Southern family. I consider myself to be very fortunate because the Getz family is not only made up of wonderful cooks, but they are self-proclaimed "foodies." Anytime we gather together, there is a lot of laughter and lots of great food, including many versions of corn bread. Gatherings always include berry picking, fishing, golf, Farmers' Markets, and any roadside hot boiled peanut stand we can find. While many southerners consider corn bread with sugar in it to be a "Yankee" corn bread, we like ALL kinds of corn bread. This one has sugar and whole corn kernels in it for an added boost in flavor. It is a moist, somewhat "cakey" bread that is quick to put together. We like this recipe best served piping hot with honey butter.

1. Place all ingredients in the order listed into the bread maker; close lid.

2. Press MENU and select QUICK.

3. Press COLOR and select DARK.

4. Press START.

5. After 5 minutes, press and hold PAUSE until machine stops; check if ingredients are uniformly mixed and use a spatula to scrape the sides; close lid and hold PAUSE to resume mixing.

6. Total machine time is 2 hours and 10 minutes.

Poppyseed Bread

Makes 1 cake

Ingredients

1 cup unsalted butter, softened
1½ cups granulated sugar
1 can (12.5 ounces) poppy seed filling
4 large eggs
1 teaspoon vanilla extract

1 cup sour cream
¼ teaspoon butter vanilla extract (see source page)
2½ cups unbleached all purpose flour
2 teaspoons baking powder
1 teaspoon kosher salt

When my boys were little, my friend Susanna and I joined the local Quilters' Guild. It was a wonderful group of ladies who came together to quilt and talk about faith, farming, families and food. One day, when I was leaving, a shy, Mennonite lady pressed this recipe into my hand because she thought I would really enjoy it. I don't remember her name, but this recipe is amazing. I have adapted it for the bread machine's CAKE cycle and have added a bit of my favorite butter vanilla extract.

1. Place all ingredients in the order listed into the bread maker; close lid.

2. Press MENU and select CAKE.

3. Press COLOR and select DARK.

4. Press START.

5. After 5 minutes, press and hold PAUSE until machine stops; check if ingredients are uniformly mixed and use a spatula to scrape the sides; close lid and hold PAUSE to resume mixing.

6. After 1 hour and 50 minutes, the baking cycle is complete; immediately press and hold the STOP button until the machine beeps.

7. Press MENU and select BAKE.

8. Press TIME and set to 20 minutes.

9. Press START (this bread is one of the few recipes that require additional baking time).

Mama Claire's Spoon Bread

Makes 1 loaf

Ingredients

½ cup (1 stick) unsalted butter, softened
1 cup corn kernels
1 cup corn meal
1 cup onions, chopped
1 teaspoon hot sauce (optional)
2 tablespoons yellow mustard
2 tablespoons kosher salt

4 large eggs
2 egg whites
2 cups milk
⅔ cup unbleached all purpose flour
½ cup Parmesan cheese, grated
½ teaspoon ground black pepper

Mama Claire, my charming mother-in-law, is a wonderful lady and an excellent cook. She gave me this recipe when I was first dating Greg. She helped me understand the style of cooking Greg grew up with and has shared many recipes, tips and laughter with me over the years. Not only had I never been to the South, but I had never cooked any Southern dishes before. Now I cannot imagine life without a huge repertoire of Southern recipes. All family gatherings include this delectable and tender spoon bread, as well as fried chicken and gallons of sweet tea.

1. Place all ingredients in the order listed into the bread maker; close lid.

2. Press MENU and select QUICK.

3. Press COLOR and select DARK.

4. Press START.

5. After 5 minutes, press and hold PAUSE until machine stops; check if ingredients are uniformly mixed and use a spatula to scrape the sides; close lid and hold PAUSE to resume mixing.

6. Total machine time is 2 hours and 10 minutes.

Marian's Tip:
A great compliment to this bread is my pepper jelly (the recipe is on page 154).

Zucchini Bread

Makes 1 loaf

Ingredients

3 cups zucchini, shredded
1½ cups granulated sugar
6 tablespoons unsalted butter, softened
2 large eggs
¼ cup sour cream
1 tablespoon lemon juice

2 cups unbleached all purpose flour
1 teaspoon baking soda
1 teaspoon baking powder
¼ teaspoon ground cinnamon
1¼ teaspoons kosher salt
½ cup pecan pieces

Anyone who grows zucchini in their vegetable garden knows that it is a good idea to have lots of recipes that call for zucchini and plenty of hungry friends to share them with. It just seems to grow and grow! I am sure that is how one smart person developed a quick bread recipe calling for zucchini. A family favorite, this loaf, which keeps well and freezes beautifully, is unbelievably moist and pretty with a delicious flavor. Each time I make a batch, I hope to have some leftovers for breakfast the next day - it never seems to make it that long.

1. Place zucchini on a kitchen towel and squeeze to remove excess water.

2. Place all ingredients in the order listed into the bread maker; close lid.

3. Press MENU and select QUICK.

4. Press COLOR and select DARK.

5. Press START.

6. After 5 minutes, press and hold PAUSE until machine stops; check if ingredients are uniformly mixed and use a spatula to scrape the sides; close lid and hold PAUSE to resume mixing.

7. Total machine time is 2 hours and 10 minutes.

Marian's Tip:
Be sure to really squeeze the water out of the zucchini. If you skip this step, the bread will have a gummy texture and be less flavorful.

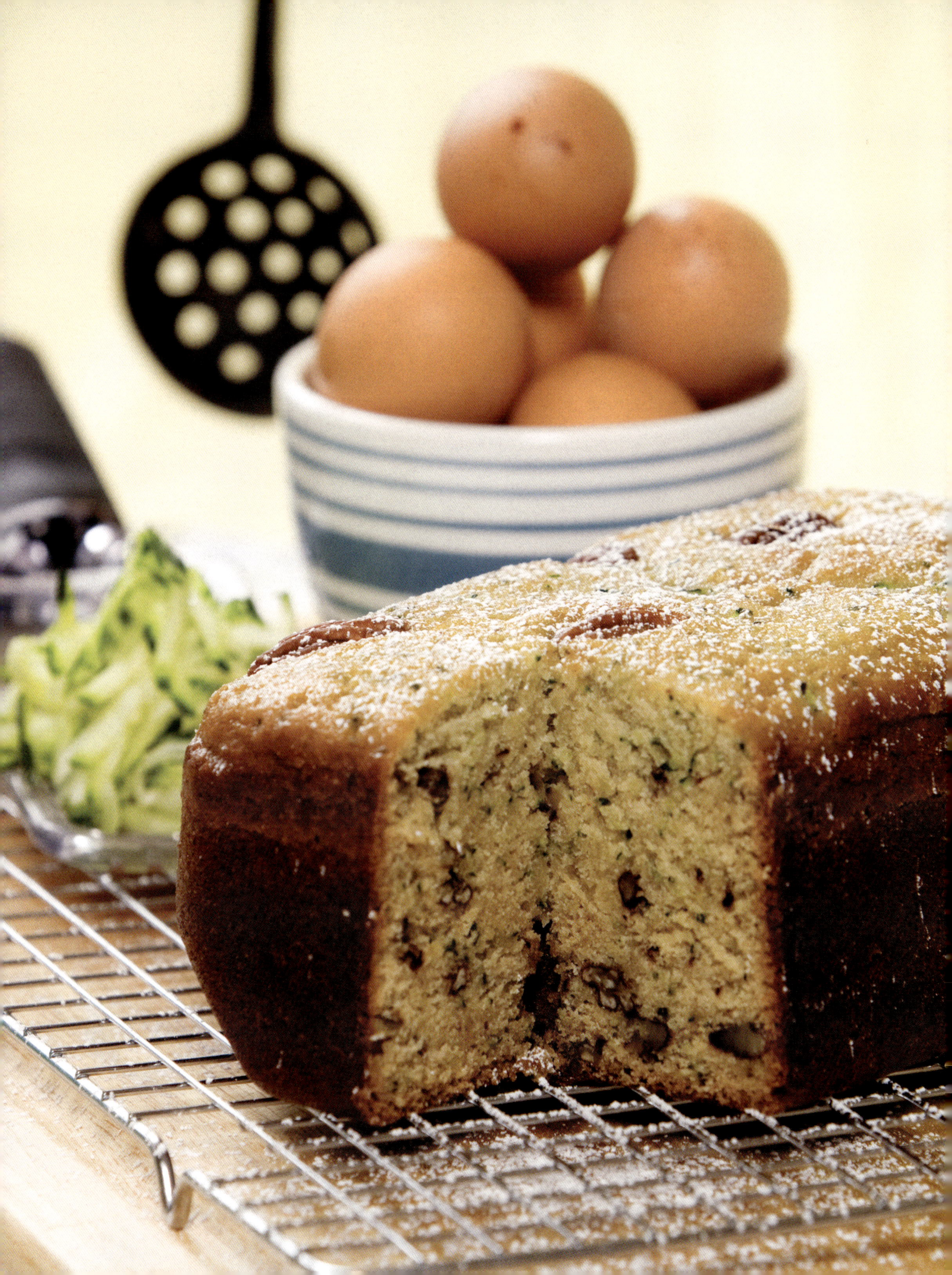

My Favorite Banana Bread

Makes 1 loaf

Ingredients

4 large overripe bananas, sliced
2 large eggs
½ cup (1 stick) unsalted butter, softened
1 teaspoon pure vanilla extract
3 tablespoons sour cream

2 cups unbleached all purpose flour
1 cup sugar
1 teaspoon baking soda
½ teaspoon baking powder
½ teaspoon kosher salt

Banana bread is one of my favorite foods of all time. Back in the Congo, Africa, bananas were plentiful and grew year-round. We did not gather or buy bananas by the bunch or hand like we do here in America, but by the entire stalk. A stalk could easily have 100 or more bananas on it. Imagine trying to eat that many bananas as fast as they ripened. This recipe came about because of this over abundance. This bread has the most bananas in each loaf of any recipe I know. Not only will it stay fresh for several days, but it also freezes very well.

1. Place all ingredients in the order listed into the bread maker; close lid.

2. Press MENU and select CAKE.

3. Press COLOR and select DARK.

4. Press START.

5. After 5 minutes, press and hold PAUSE until machine stops; check if ingredients are uniformly mixed and use a spatula to scrape the sides; close lid and hold PAUSE to resume mixing.

6. Total machine time is 1 hour and 50 minutes.

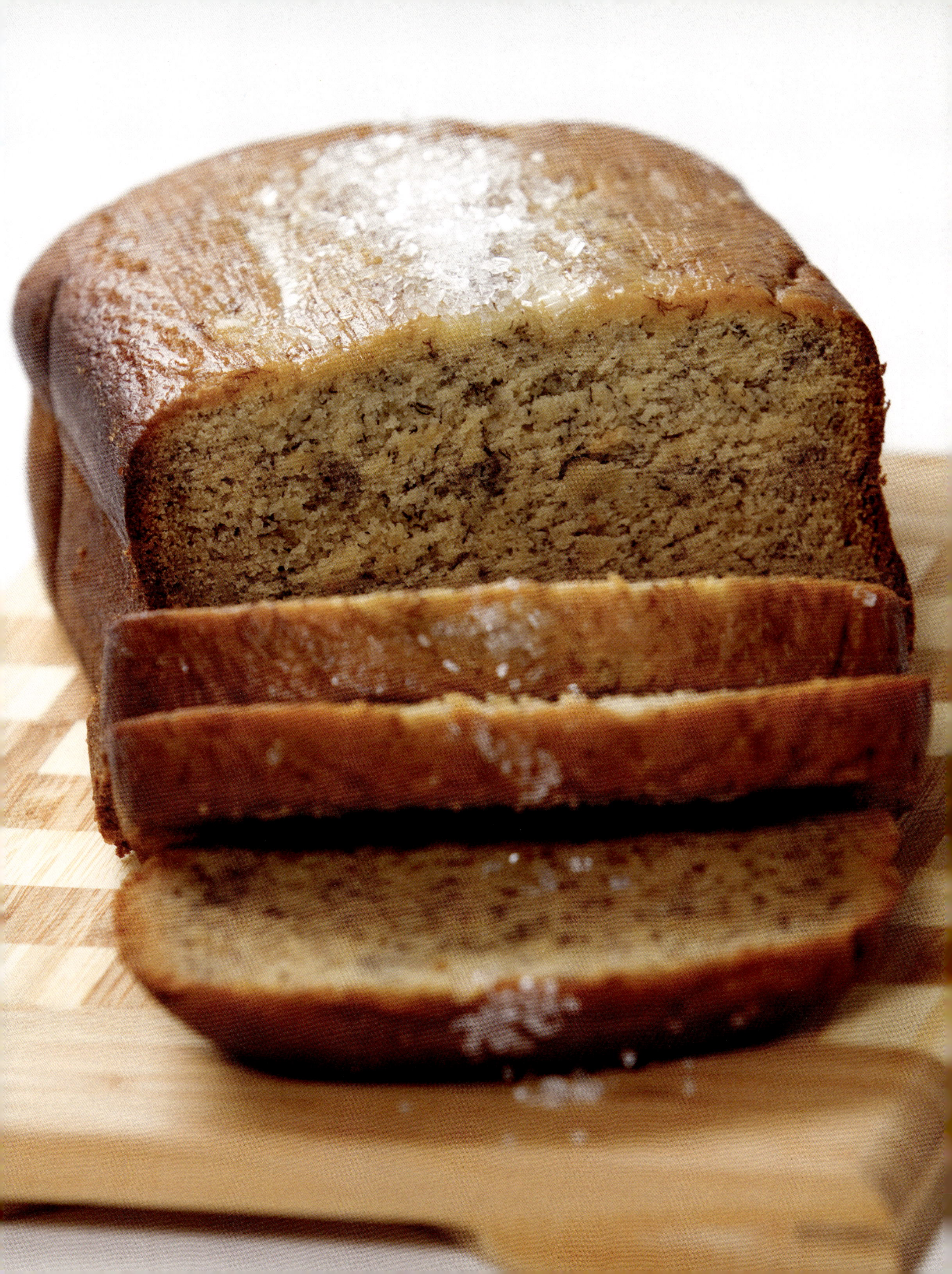

Blueberry Lemon Quick Bread

Makes 1 loaf

Ingredients

½ cup (1 stick) unsalted butter, softened
½ cup heavy whipping cream
½ cup water
1 cup granulated sugar
2 large eggs
Zest of 1 lemon
1 tablespoon fresh lemon juice
1⅓ cups fresh blueberries, tossed in 1 tablespoon flour
¾ cup pecan pieces
2 cups unbleached all purpose flour
1½ teaspoons baking powder
1 teaspoon kosher salt
1 teaspoon vanilla extract

Glaze

1½ cups powdered sugar
1 tablespoon fresh lemon juice
1 tablespoon water

Blueberries are Greg's favorite type of berry and we go blueberry picking as often as possible. We enjoy the good company as much as the berries themselves. This recipe is just divine. Whenever I make this bread, Greg always asks me to be extra generous with the pecans.

1. Place all ingredients in the order listed into the bread maker; close lid.

2. Press MENU and select QUICK.

3. Press COLOR and select DARK.

4. Press START.

5. After 5 minutes, press and hold PAUSE until machine stops; check if ingredients are uniformly mixed and use a spatula to scrape the sides; close lid and hold PAUSE to resume mixing.

6. Total machine time is 2 hours and 10 minutes.

7. In a bowl, combine glaze ingredients and pour it over the warm bread.

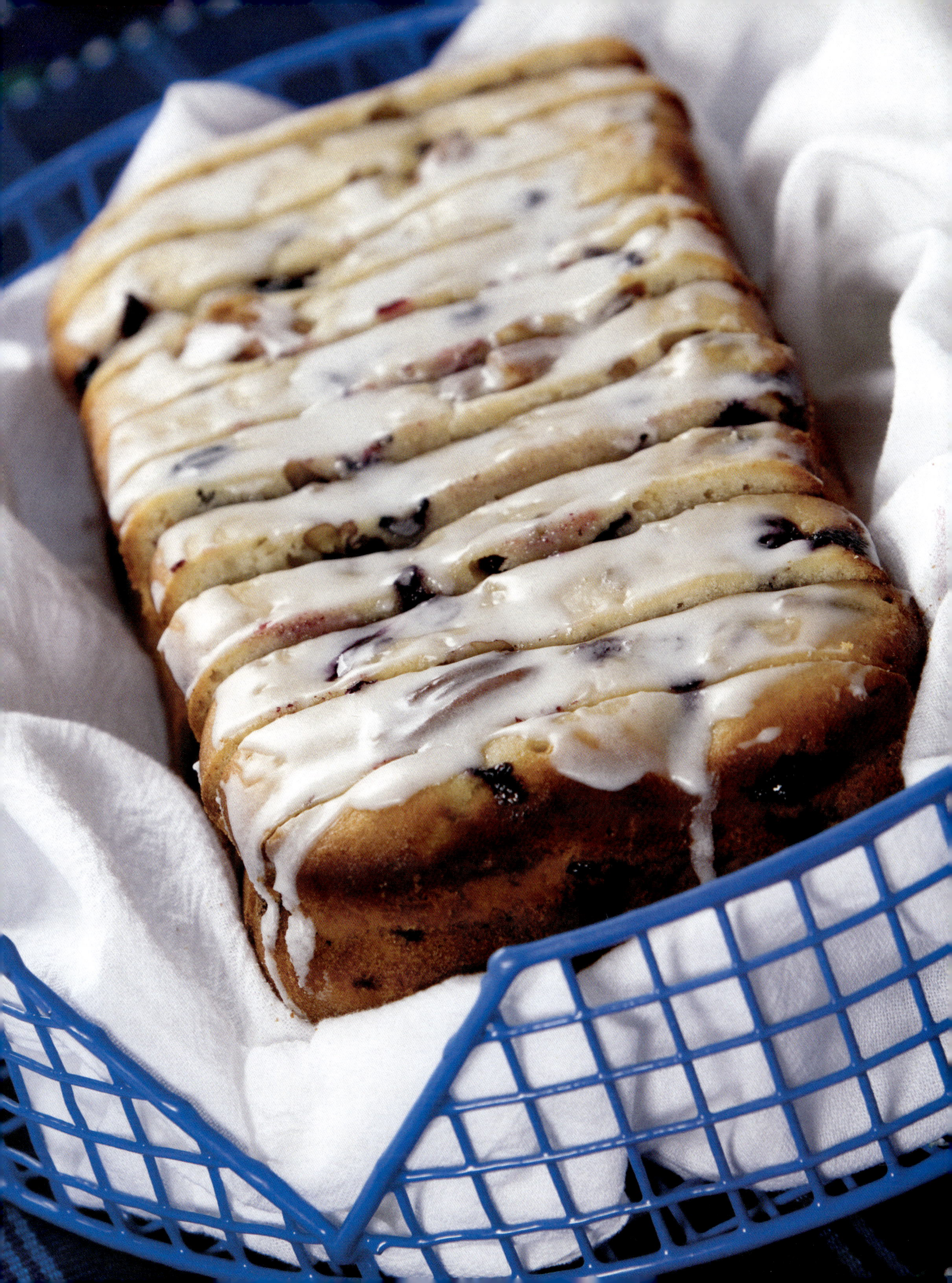

Cranberry Orange Quick Bread

Makes 1 loaf

Ingredients

1½ cups fresh cranberries, chopped
1 large egg
Zest from 1 orange
⅓ cup orange juice
6 tablespoons unsalted butter, softened
⅔ cup buttermilk

2 cups unbleached all purpose flour
1 cup granulated sugar
1 teaspoon kosher salt
1 tablespoon baking powder
½ cup pecans, toasted

I love how the house smells when cranberry orange bread is baking. It is in the family of recipes that just smell like the holidays. It makes a great gift for family and friends, especially with a jar of homemade jam.

1. Place all ingredients in the order listed into the bread maker; close lid.

2. Press MENU and select QUICK.

3. Press COLOR and select DARK.

4. Press START.

5. After 5 minutes, press and hold PAUSE until machine stops; check if ingredients are uniformly mixed and use a spatula to scrape the sides; close lid and hold PAUSE to resume mixing.

6. Total machine time is 2 hours and 10 minutes.

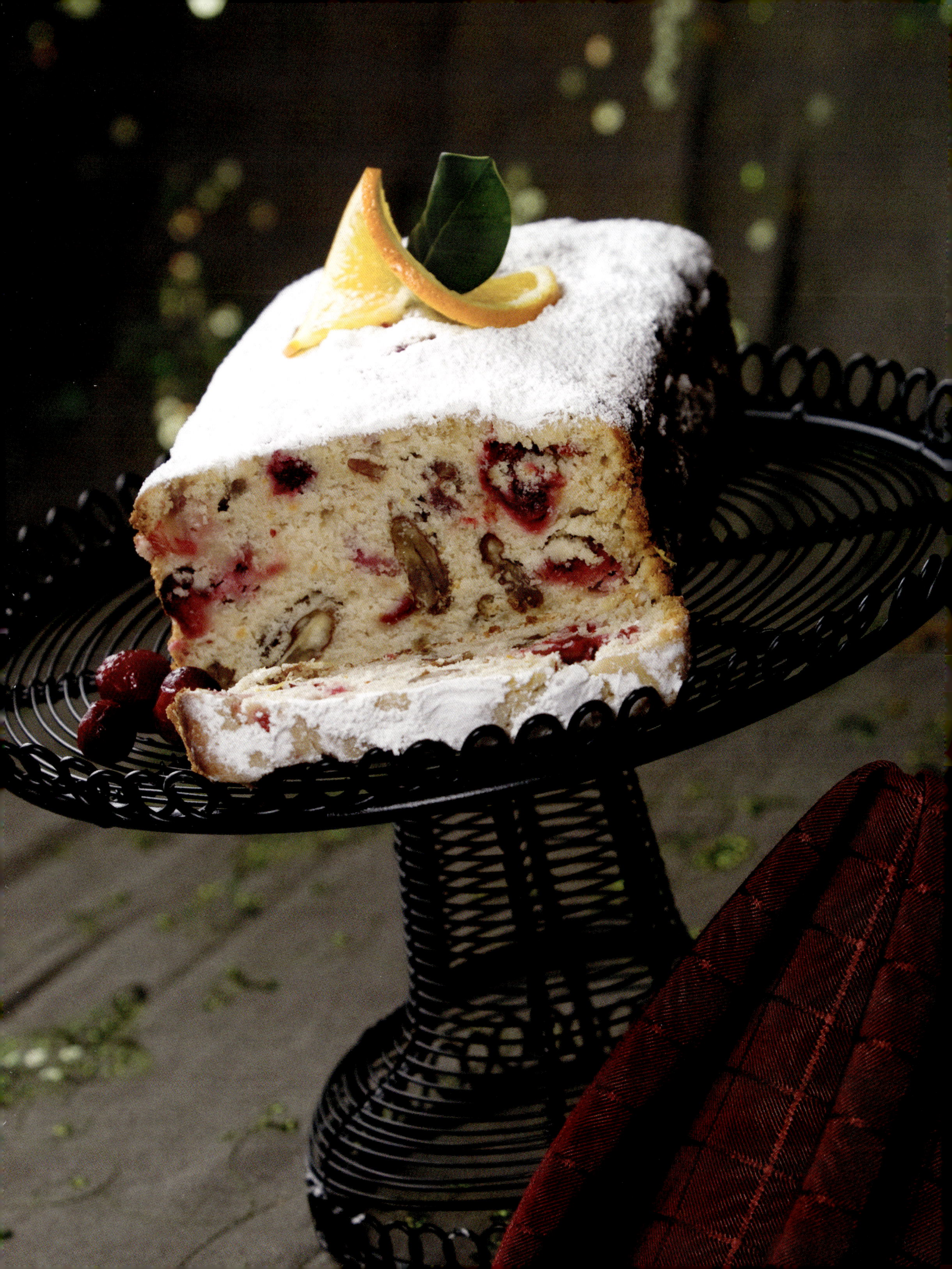

Sour Cream Coffee Cake

Makes 1 loaf

Batter Ingredients

¾ cup unsalted butter, softened
1¼ cups granulated sugar
¾ cup sour cream
2 large eggs
2 teaspoons pure vanilla extract
1¼ cups unbleached all purpose flour
1 teaspoon baking powder
1 teaspoon kosher salt

Streusel Ingredients

⅓ cup packed light brown sugar
2 teaspoons unbleached all purpose flour
2 teaspoons ground cinnamon

I was fortunate to receive the sour cream coffee cake recipe as a wedding shower gift from a family friend. It is one that I love to take when we are invited over to a friend's home. It is one of those recipes that I make over and over again, especially when my kids come to visit. Like most recipes that have sour cream in them, it is so tender and flavorful.

1. Place all batter ingredients in the order listed into the bread maker; close lid.

2. Press MENU and select CAKE.

3. Press COLOR and select DARK.

4. Press START.

5. Set a kitchen timer for 30 minutes.

6. To make the streusel, combine streusel ingredients in a small bowl; mix well. When timer rings, sprinkle ⅓ of the streusel in a line down the center of the batter avoiding the edges of the pan.

7. Using a spoon, lift batter up and over the top of the streusel, trying to cover it with batter.

8. Sprinkle remaining streusel over the top of the cake and close the lid.

9. Total machine time is 1 hour and 50 minutes.

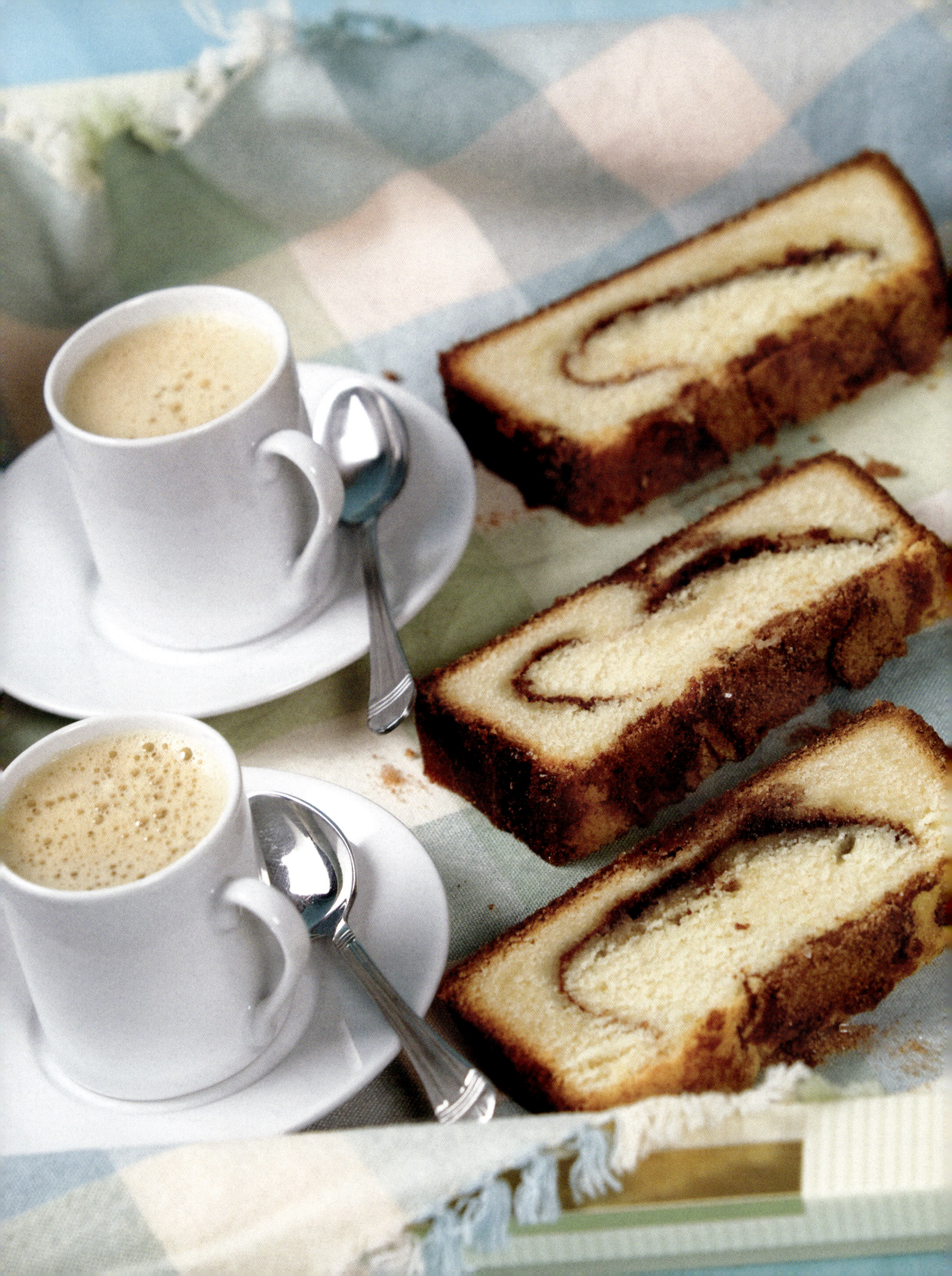

Pumpkin Bread

Makes 1 loaf

Ingredients

2 large eggs
1¼ cups pumpkin puree
1 cup packed light brown sugar
⅓ cup unsalted butter, softened
⅓ cup vegetable oil
1 tablespoon Apple Pie Spice (a mixture of cinnamon, nutmeg and allspice)

1 teaspoon baking soda
1 teaspoon kosher salt
1 teaspoon vanilla extract
1 teaspoon apple cider vinegar
1¾ cups unbleached all purpose flour

Streusel Topping

½ cup packed light brown sugar
2 tablespoons unbleached all purpose flour
1 tablespoon ground cinnamon

Pinch of kosher salt
2 tablespoons unsalted butter, softened

This pumpkin bread recipe has all of the flavors and aroma of pumpkin pie. Since this loaf is very moist and freezes well, it is perfect as a gift or for taking it to a covered-dish supper. You can use freshly cooked or canned pumpkin. If you can find Kabocha squash (a Japanese orange-fleshed squash) you will find that it makes this recipe especially sweet and delicious.

1. Place all ingredients in the order listed into the bread maker; close lid.

2. Press MENU and select QUICK.

3. Press COLOR and select DARK.

4. Press START.

5. After 5 minutes, press and hold PAUSE until machine stops; check if ingredients are uniformly mixed and use a spatula to scrape the sides; close lid and hold PAUSE to resume mixing.

6. In a bowl, combine streusel ingredients; mix well.

7. One hour into the baking cycle, sprinkle streusel evenly over the top of the batter; close lid.

8. Total machine time is 2 hours and 10 minutes.

Gingerbread Cake

Makes 1 cake

Ingredients

1 cup buttermilk
½ cup unsalted butter, softened
¾ cup molasses
1 large egg
¾ cup packed light brown sugar
½ teaspoon baking soda

1 tablespoon ground ginger
1 teaspoon ground cinnamon
½ teaspoon ground nutmeg
1 teaspoon ground clove
1¾ cups unbleached all purpose flour
1 teaspoon kosher salt

Sheer Lemon Sauce

⅔ cup granulated sugar
2 tablespoons cornstarch
1 tablespoon fresh lemon zest
⅓ cup fresh lemon juice

½ cup water
4 tablespoons unsalted butter
½ teaspoon vanilla extract

This cake's warm and spicy aroma is reminiscent of the holidays. One of my favorite ways to enjoy this cake is with a small (not too small) dollop of homemade whipped cream. You can also serve it with a lemon sauce like my mother does.

1. Place all ingredients in the order listed into the bread maker; close lid.

2. Press MENU and select CAKE.

3. Press COLOR and select DARK.

4. Press START.

5. After 5 minutes, press and hold PAUSE until machine stops; check if ingredients are uniformly mixed and use a spatula to scrape the sides; close lid and hold PAUSE to resume mixing.

6. Total machine time is 1 hour and 50 minutes.

7. In a saucepan over medium heat, combine all sauce ingredients and bring to a boil; whisk constantly and serve with warm cake.

Jordan & Ben's Brownies

Makes 12 to 16 brownies

Ingredients

1 cup unsalted butter, softened
2 cups granulated sugar
4 large eggs
¼ teaspoon kosher salt

1 teaspoon vanilla extract
½ cup good quality cocoa
1 cup unbleached all purpose flour

This brownie's short ingredient list coupled with the hands-free ease of mixing and baking them in the bread maker is a great way to make homemade treats in today's hectic lifestyle. I first developed this recipe when my boys, Jordan and Ben, were really young. I used to first melt the butter so that their precious little hands could easily stir the batter for these brownies. The trick to sharing the mixing task was that once you took a lick of the batter, you had to pass the bowl to your brother for a turn at stirring. I have always loved cooking with my family. Being together in the kitchen is my idea of a perfect day. The secret to this easy recipe is the cocoa. Use a good quality cocoa. Sadly, the grocery stores rarely carry the quality you need for this recipe. I suggest ordering the right cocoa online (see source page).

1. Place all ingredients in the order listed into the bread maker; close lid.

2. Press MENU and select CAKE.

3. Press COLOR and select DARK.

4. Press START.

5. After 5 minutes, press and hold PAUSE until machine stops; check if ingredients are uniformly mixed and use a spatula to scrape the sides; close lid and hold PAUSE to resume mixing.

6. Total machine time is 1 hour and 50 minutes.

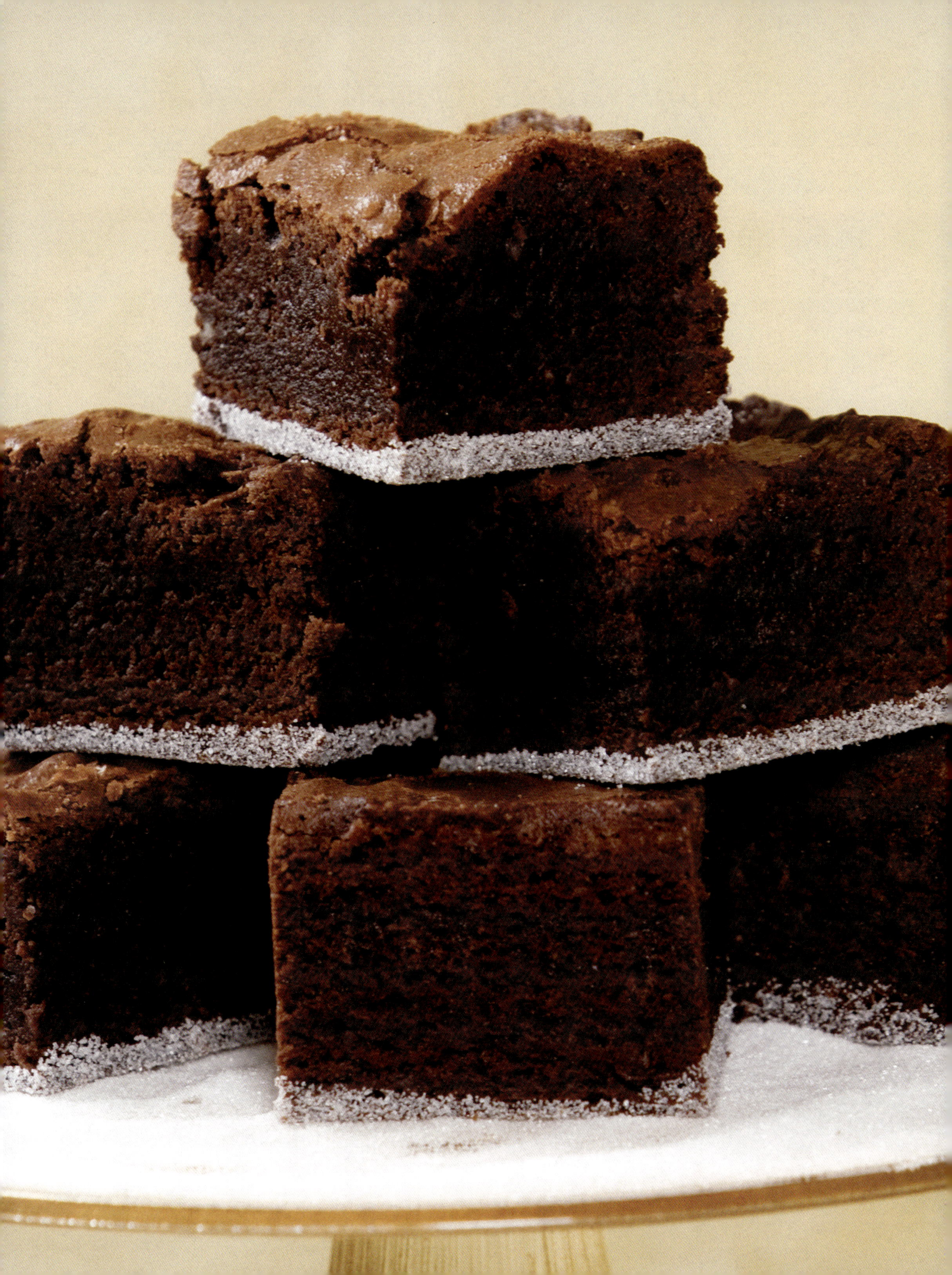

Apple Sauce Quick Bread

Makes 1 loaf

Ingredients

2 large eggs
¾ cup apple sauce
1½ cups Granny Smith, Pink Lady or Ida Red apples, unpeeled and shredded
½ cup unsalted butter, softened
2 teaspoons vanilla extract
1 cup granulated sugar
1 teaspoon baking soda
1 teaspoon baking powder
1 teaspoon kosher salt
2 teaspoons Apple Pie Spice (a mixture of cinnamon, nutmeg and allspice)
1⅔ cups unbleached all purpose flour

Cinnamon Glaze

1½ cups powdered sugar
½ teaspoon ground cinnamon
1 tablespoon lemon juice
1 tablespoon water

Quick breads are called "quick" because they do not contain yeast, which is relatively slow to rise. Instead, quick breads are leavened or raised by baking powder or baking soda. Apple sauce quick bread is easy to make, very moist and extremely flavorful. People always ask me for the recipe and I strongly suggest using really fragrant apples when making this bread.

1. Place all ingredients in the order listed into the bread maker; close lid.

2. Press MENU and select QUICK.

3. Press COLOR and select DARK.

4. Press START.

5. After 5 minutes, press and hold PAUSE until machine stops; check if ingredients are uniformly mixed and use a spatula to scrape the sides; close lid and hold PAUSE to resume mixing.

6. Total machine time is 2 hours and 10 minutes.

7. In a bowl, combine glaze ingredients; mix well and pour over cooled bread.

Cakes & Frostings

Carrot Cake 86
Coconut Cake 88
Coconut Cake Frosting 90
Sticky Toffee Pudding Cake 91
Easy Vanilla Yellow Cake 92
Oatmeal Cake 94
Chocolate Ganache Icing 96
Classic Pound Cake 97
Glazed Cream Cheese Pound Cake 98
Wolf's Lemon Pound Cake 100
My Favorite Chocolate Pound Cake 102
Billowy Seven Minute Frosting 103
Easy Moist Chocolate Cake 104
Chocolate Whipped Cream Frosting 106
Glaze for Chocolate Crazy Cake 107
Chocolate Crazy Cake 108
Southern Red Velvet Cake 110
Southern Red Velvet Cake Icing 112

Carrot Cake

Makes 1 cake

Ingredients

2 large eggs
½ cup vegetable oil
1⅓ cups sugar
1 cup carrot, pureed
½ cup pineapple, pureed
1½ teaspoons kosher salt

1 tablespoon ground cinnamon
2 cups unbleached all purpose flour
1 teaspoon baking soda
1 teaspoon baking powder
2 teaspoons vanilla extract

Icing

1½ cups powdered sugar
¼ cup cream cheese, softened

2 tablespoons unsalted butter, softened
½ teaspoon vanilla extract

One day, when I was icing up a carrot cake at the café, a burly line cook named Bulldog asked for a taste. He thought my carrot cake was bland and did not like it at all. I tweaked the recipe by adding pineapple which made it much better. As I was grinding the carrots and pineapple to make another carrot cake, I accidentally knocked over a 5 gallon bucket of honey. The honey was all over my clogs, the prep kitchen floor, the flour bins and the dish area. It was a mess! When I got it all cleaned up, I realized the food processor was still running. I used the carrots and pineapple, which now looked like very fine baby food, to finish the cake. To my amazement, it was the best tasting carrot cake yet. I still make my carrot cake that way, though it really only takes a minute to puree the carrots and pineapple.

1. Place all cake ingredients in the order listed into the bread maker; close lid.

2. Press MENU and select CAKE.

3. Press COLOR and select DARK.

4. Press START.

5. After 5 minutes, press and hold PAUSE until machine stops; check if ingredients are uniformly mixed and use a spatula to scrape the sides; close lid and hold PAUSE to resume mixing.

6. Total machine time is 2 hours and 10 minutes.

7. In a bowl, combine icing ingredients and spread over the cake.

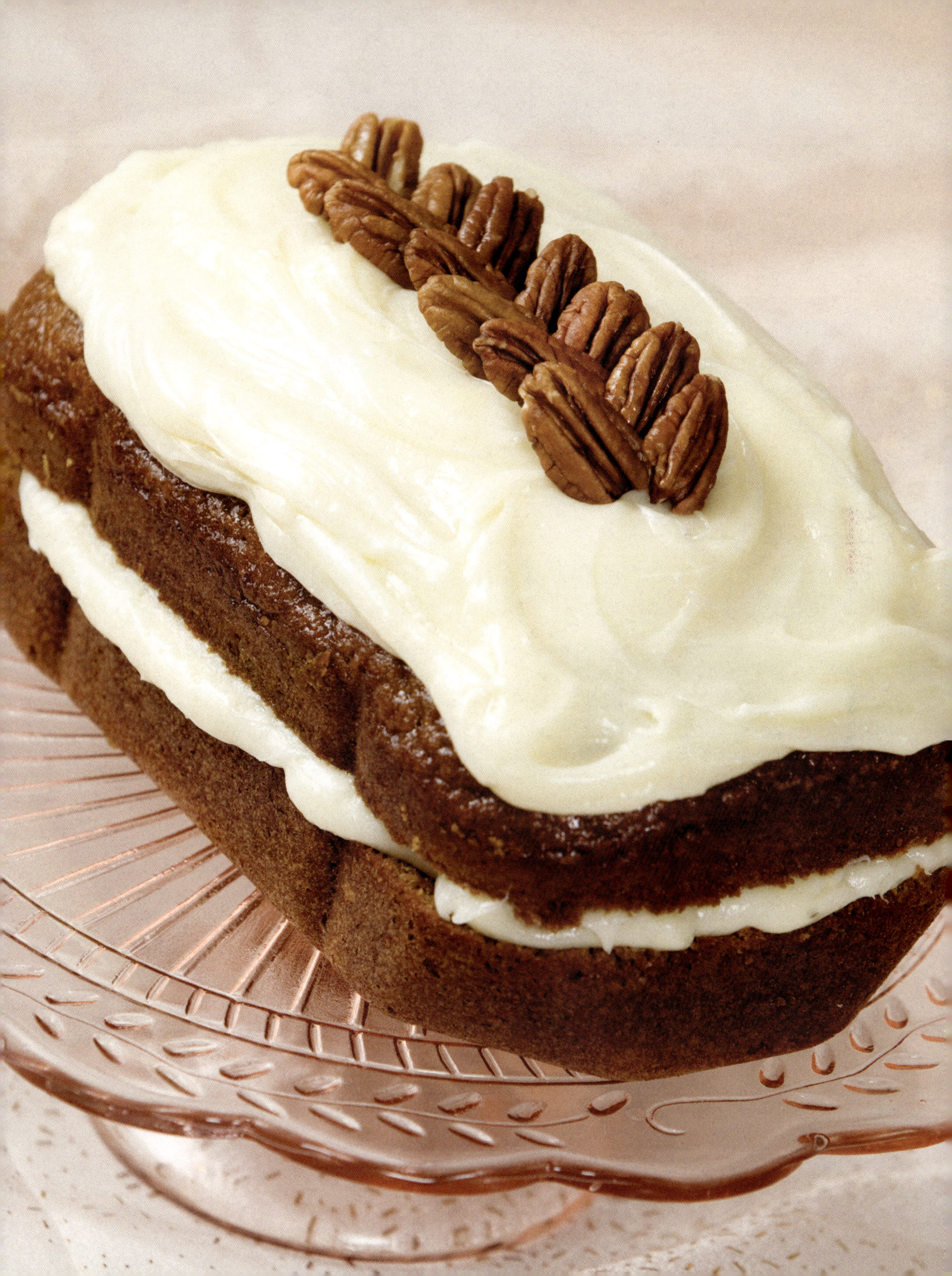

Coconut Cake

Makes 1 cake

Ingredients

4 large eggs
¾ cup cream of coconut
¼ cup water
1 teaspoon coconut extract
1 teaspoon vanilla extract
¾ cup (1½ sticks) unsalted butter, softened
2¼ cups cake flour
1 cup granulated sugar
1 tablespoon baking powder
1 teaspoon kosher salt

I love coconut! In Africa, we had as much fresh coconut as we wanted. We primarily used it in savory dishes rather than in sweet ones. Coconut cake is exceptionally moist and gets better as it sits. I use a canned cream of coconut product that you can find in either the Spanish section of your grocery store or in the aisle where the mixed drink items (piña coladas) are. The can holds 15 ounces and after you make the cake and the icing, you will have about ⅓ cup leftover. I like to use the leftovers to spread between the cake layers before I ice the cake. It not only soaks into the cake, but it also boosts the coconut flavor.

1. Place all ingredients in the order listed into the bread maker; close lid.

2. Press MENU and select CAKE.

3. Press COLOR and select DARK.

4. Press START.

5. After 5 minutes, press and hold PAUSE until machine stops; check if ingredients are uniformly mixed and use a spatula to scrape the sides; close lid and hold PAUSE to resume mixing.

6. Total machine time is 1 hour and 50 minutes.

7. Cool cake completely and split in half horizontally to make 2 layers; spread ⅓ cup of the leftover cream of coconut between the layers before frosting (see frosting on page 90).

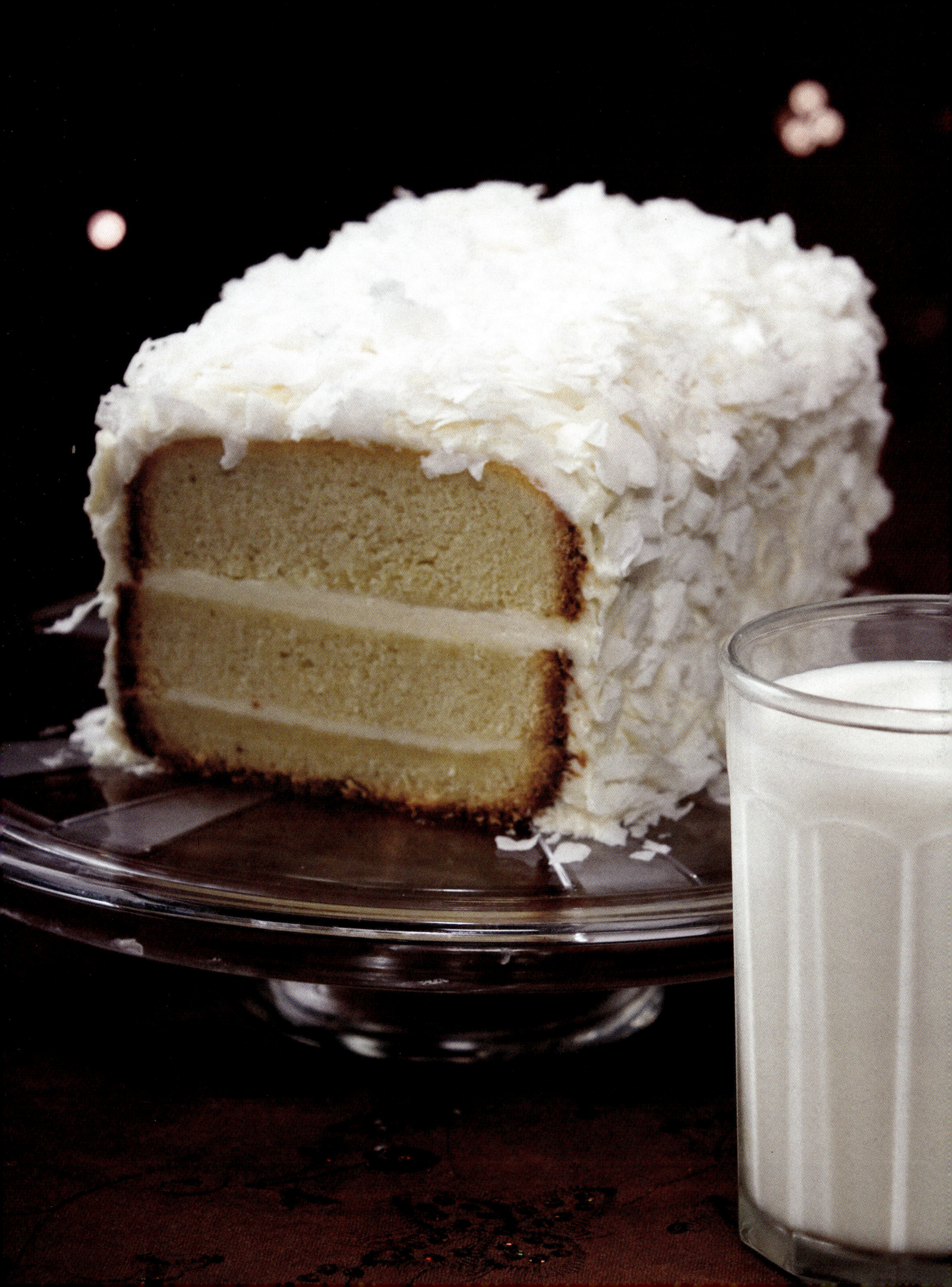

Coconut Cake Frosting

Ingredients

2 tablespoons heavy whipping cream
1 teaspoon coconut extract
1 teaspoon vanilla extract
⅛ teaspoon kosher salt
1 cup unsalted butter, softened
¼ cup cream of coconut
3 cups powdered sugar
1 cup shredded unsweetened coconut for topping (optional)

This frosting is excellent on the coconut cake. It uses up the last bits of the cream of coconut called for in the cake recipe so there is no waste. This is a simple stir-together recipe that has big coconut flavor.

1. In a bowl, combine all ingredients.

2. Using a whisk, mix until light and fluffy.

3. Spread frosting on cooled coconut cake.

Sticky Toffee Pudding Cake

Makes 1 cake

Ingredients

1 cup dates, chopped
1 cup water
1 teaspoon baking soda
¼ cup unsalted butter, softened
¾ cup granulated sugar
2 large eggs

2 teaspoons vanilla
1 teaspoon fresh lemon juice
1½ cups unbleached all purpose flour
1 teaspoon baking powder
1 teaspoon kosher salt

Glaze

1 cup packed light brown sugar
2 tablespoons unsalted butter
½ cup heavy cream

2 tablespoons brandy
⅛ teaspoon kosher salt

This cake originated in England, where they have a penchant for calling all desserts "puddings." While the moistness in this cake comes from dates, their flavor is subtle enough that most people are not even aware that dates are in this recipe. The glaze is delightful because of the combination of cream, brown sugar and brandy, which create a decidedly butterscotch flavor.

1. In a microwave safe bowl, combine dates, water and baking soda; microwave until dates are tender.

2. Place dates and remaining ingredients into the bread maker; close lid.

3. Press MENU and select CAKE.

4. Press COLOR and select DARK.

5. Press START.

6. After 5 minutes, press and hold PAUSE until machine stops; check if ingredients are uniformly mixed and use a spatula to scrape the sides; close lid and hold PAUSE to resume mixing.

7. Total machine time is 1 hour and 50 minutes.

8. In a saucepan over medium heat, combine glaze ingredients; bring to a boil and pour over warm cake.

Easy Vanilla Yellow Cake

Makes 1 cake

Ingredients

¾ cup unsalted (1½ sticks) butter, softened
1¼ cups granulated sugar
3 large eggs
1½ teaspoons vanilla extract
½ teaspoon butter vanilla extract (see source page)
1 cup whole milk
¾ cup unbleached all purpose flour
1 cup cake flour
2½ teaspoons baking powder
1 teaspoon kosher salt

This is another easy but great recipe for your bread maker. When someone requests a yellow cake for a birthday, this is the cake I most often make. I love the look of a loaf-shaped cake that is iced and decorated. Since you just cut this cake into bread shaped slices, it is the easiest cake to serve. I love this one, split in half, filled with sliced strawberries then iced with sweetened strawberry flavored whipped cream.

1. Place all ingredients in the order listed into the bread maker; close lid.

2. Press MENU and select CAKE.

3. Press COLOR and select DARK.

4. Press START.

5. After 5 minutes, press and hold PAUSE until machine stops; check if ingredients are uniformly mixed and use a spatula to scrape the sides; close lid and hold PAUSE to resume mixing.

6. Total machine time is 1 hour and 50 minutes.

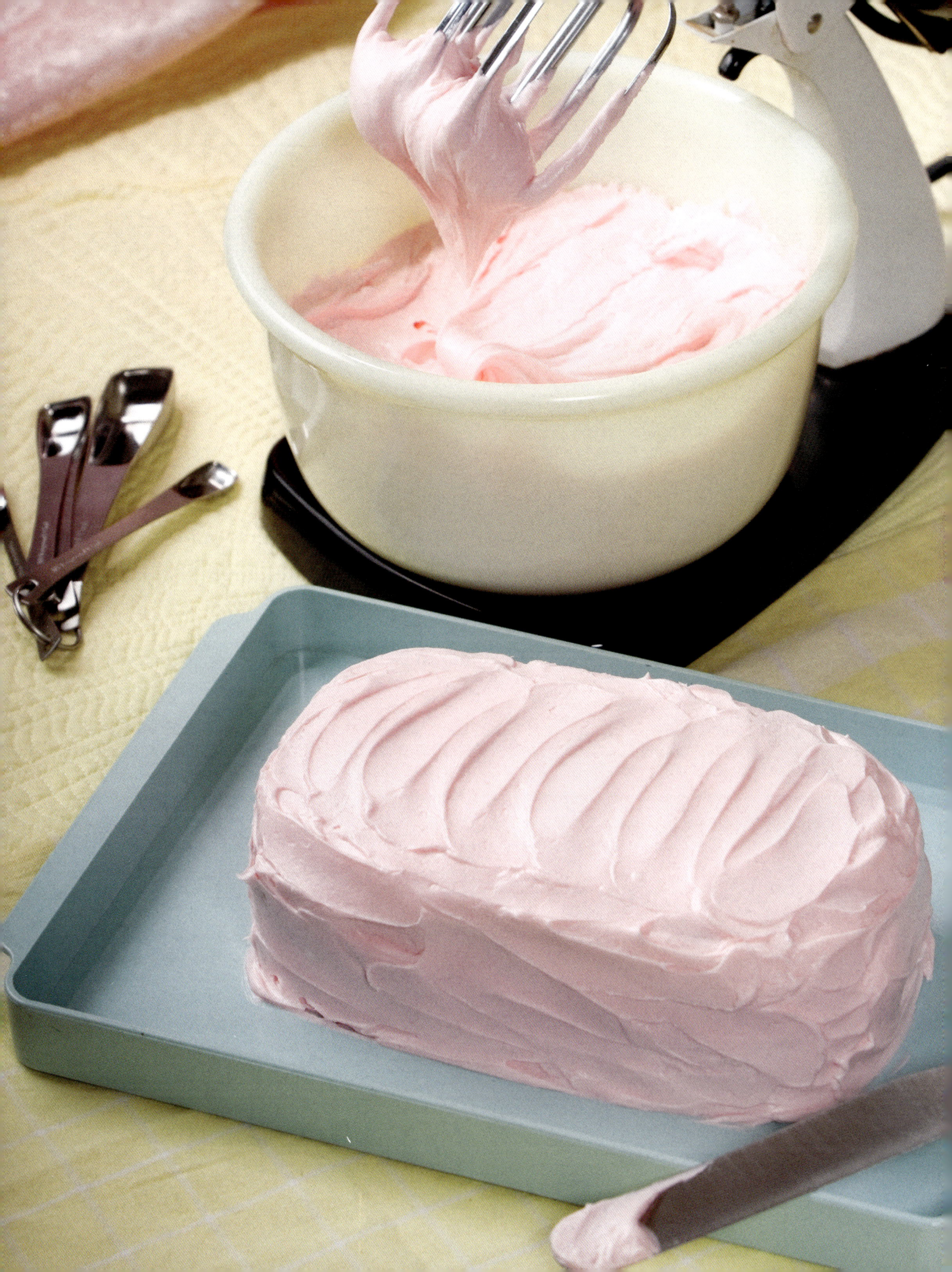

Oatmeal Cake

Makes 1 cake

Ingredients

1 cup boiling water
½ cup old fashioned rolled oats
⅓ cup unsalted butter, softened
1 cup granulated sugar
1 large egg

1 cup unbleached all purpose flour
1 teaspoon baking soda
½ teaspoon kosher salt
2 teaspoons vanilla extract

Oatmeal is such a great ingredient used in baking because it makes for unbelievable moistness with a very pleasant chewiness, which is perfect in this cake. This recipe is from my grandmother and is utterly delicious. I know you will enjoy it as much as I do.

1. Place oatmeal into the bread maker and pour boiling water over it.

2. Add butter and sugar to the bread maker; stir and let rest for 10 minutes.

3. Add remaining ingredients to the bread maker; close lid.

4. Press MENU and select CAKE.

5. Press COLOR and select DARK.

6. Press START.

7. After 5 minutes, press and hold PAUSE until machine stops; check if ingredients are uniformly mixed and use a spatula to scrape the sides; close lid and hold PAUSE to resume mixing.

8. Total machine time is 1 hour and 50 minutes.

Marian's Tip:
This cake is delicious frosted with the chocolate ganache icing (see recipe on page 96).

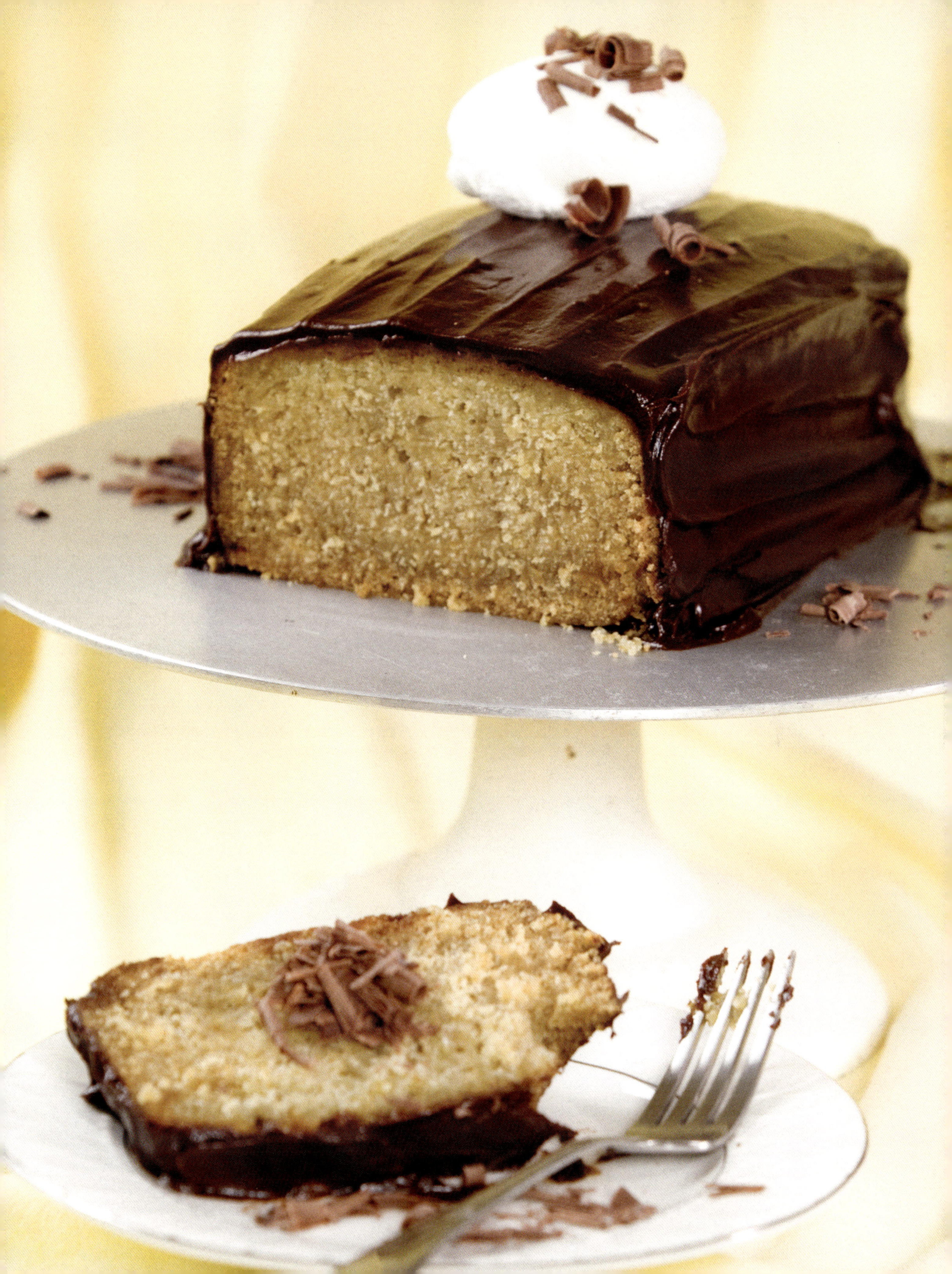

Chocolate Ganache Icing

Makes 2½ cups

Ingredients

1½ cups heavy whipping cream
3 cups good quality semi sweet chocolate chips

Not only is this is the easiest icing recipe that I know, but it is very versatile and one of the most delicious! It is my favorite glaze for donuts and éclairs, the perfect icing for ice cream and if you use it while still warm, it is fantastic as a shiny glaze for cakes. You can even turn it into a chocolate mousse by chilling it a bit and whipping it in a mixer. You can add various flavorings to it such as brandy, vanilla, orange zest or even toasted nuts to change. It is remarkably delicious.

1. In a large microwave safe bowl, bring cream to a simmer (about 4 minutes depending on your microwave).

2. Carefully pour chocolate chips into hot cream; let rest for 1 minute.

3. Whisk until smooth and shiny; mixture thickens as it cools.

4. Use it warm and pour it over a cake or chill it slightly to create a more fudgy consistency.

Classic Pound Cake

Makes 1 cake

Ingredients

6 large eggs
¾ cup unsalted butter, softened
1 cup whole milk
¼ teaspoon pure lemon oil
1 teaspoon pure vanilla extract
¼ teaspoon butter vanilla extract (see source page)

3 cups granulated sugar
3 cups unbleached all purpose flour
1 teaspoon baking powder
½ teaspoon kosher salt

This makes a tall, elegant pound cake that is perfect for any gathering. It is fine-textured, buttery and a great cake to have in your baking repertoire. The butter vanilla extract I use in this recipe is not pure, but I am over the moon for its flavor and aroma. I sneak it into many of my recipes. The smell and taste it offers reminds me of how a good, old-fashioned bakery smells like. Please see the source page for this product.

1. Place all ingredients in the order listed into the bread maker; close lid.

2. Press MENU and select CAKE.

3. Press COLOR and select DARK.

4. Press START.

5. After 5 minutes, press and hold PAUSE until machine stops; check if ingredients are uniformly mixed and use a spatula to scrape the sides; close lid and hold PAUSE to resume mixing.

6. After 1 hour and 50 minutes, the baking cycle is complete; immediately press and hold the STOP button until the machine beeps.

7. Press MENU and select BAKE.

8. Press TIME and set to 20 minutes.

9. Press START (this pound cake is one of the few recipes that require additional baking time).

Glazed Cream Cheese Pound Cake

Makes 1 loaf

Ingredients

¾ cup unsalted butter, softened
½ cup cream cheese, softened
1½ cups granulated sugar
3 large eggs

2 teaspoons pure vanilla extract
1 teaspoon kosher salt
1½ cups unbleached all purpose flour
1 teaspoon baking powder

Glaze

1½ cups powdered sugar
¼ teaspoon pure vanilla extract
1 tablespoon heavy cream
1 tablespoon water

This is my favorite pound cake - hands down! When I was the pastry chef at the Wolfgang Puck Café in Orlando, it was on the menu and was always a great hit with customers and employees alike. It has a really fine crumb and delicate taste. It stays fresh for many days and freezes nicely. I love making it in the bread maker. Simply dump in all of the ingredients and enjoy the cake. I still smile at how easy it is to make. This just happens to be one of Wolf's favorites and he enjoys a slice with a double espresso.

1. Place all ingredients in the order listed into the bread maker; close lid.

2. Press MENU and select QUICK.

3. Press START.

4. After 5 minutes, press and hold PAUSE until machine stops; check if ingredients are uniformly mixed and use a spatula to scrape the sides; close lid and hold PAUSE to resume mixing.

5. Total machine time is 2 hours and 10 minutes.

6. In a bowl, combine glaze ingredients; mix well and pour over cooled cake.

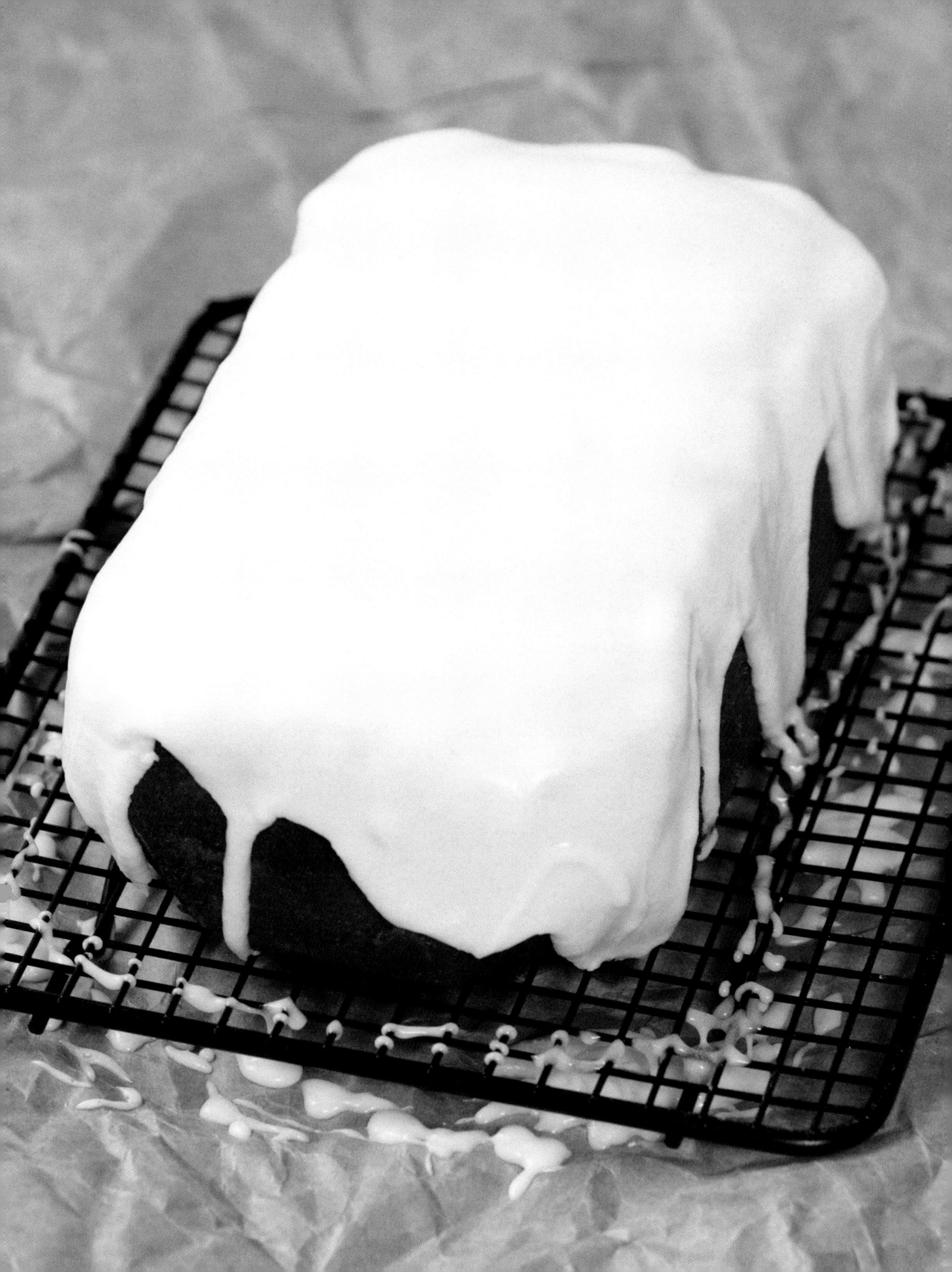

Wolf's Lemon Pound Cake

Makes 1 loaf

Ingredients

8 ounces cream cheese, softened
½ cup unsalted butter, softened
1¼ cups granulated sugar
2 large eggs
2¼ cups unbleached all purpose flour

1 tablespoon baking powder
½ teaspoon kosher salt
½ cup plain yogurt, preferably Greek
2 tablespoons fresh lemon zest
1 tablespoon fresh lemon juice

Lemon Glaze

2 cups powdered sugar
3 tablespoons fresh lemon juice
1 tablespoon fresh lemon zest
2 tablespoons water

Wolfgang loves the flavor of lemons; lemon cookies, lemon cake, lemon ice cream, lemon anything! You should see his eyes light up when he is offered a lemon dessert. Wolfgang absolutely loves this cake. When I was the pastry chef at the Wolfgang Puck Café in Orlando, we had this cake on the menu. I paired miniature squares of it with a tiny scoop of lemon gelato, a mini hot lemon soufflé and lemon curd sandwiched short bread cookies. The finished loaf here is stunning with the glaze dripping down. The lemon juice in the glaze keeps it pristine white with tiny yellow flecks from the zest.

1. Place all ingredients in the order listed into the bread maker; close lid.

2. Press MENU and select QUICK.

3. Press COLOR and select MEDIUM.

4. Press START.

5. After 5 minutes, press and hold PAUSE until machine stops; check if ingredients are uniformly mixed and use a spatula to scrape the sides; close lid and hold PAUSE to resume mixing.

6. Total machine time is 2 hours and 10 minutes.

7. In a bowl, combine glaze ingredients; mix well and pour over cooled cake.

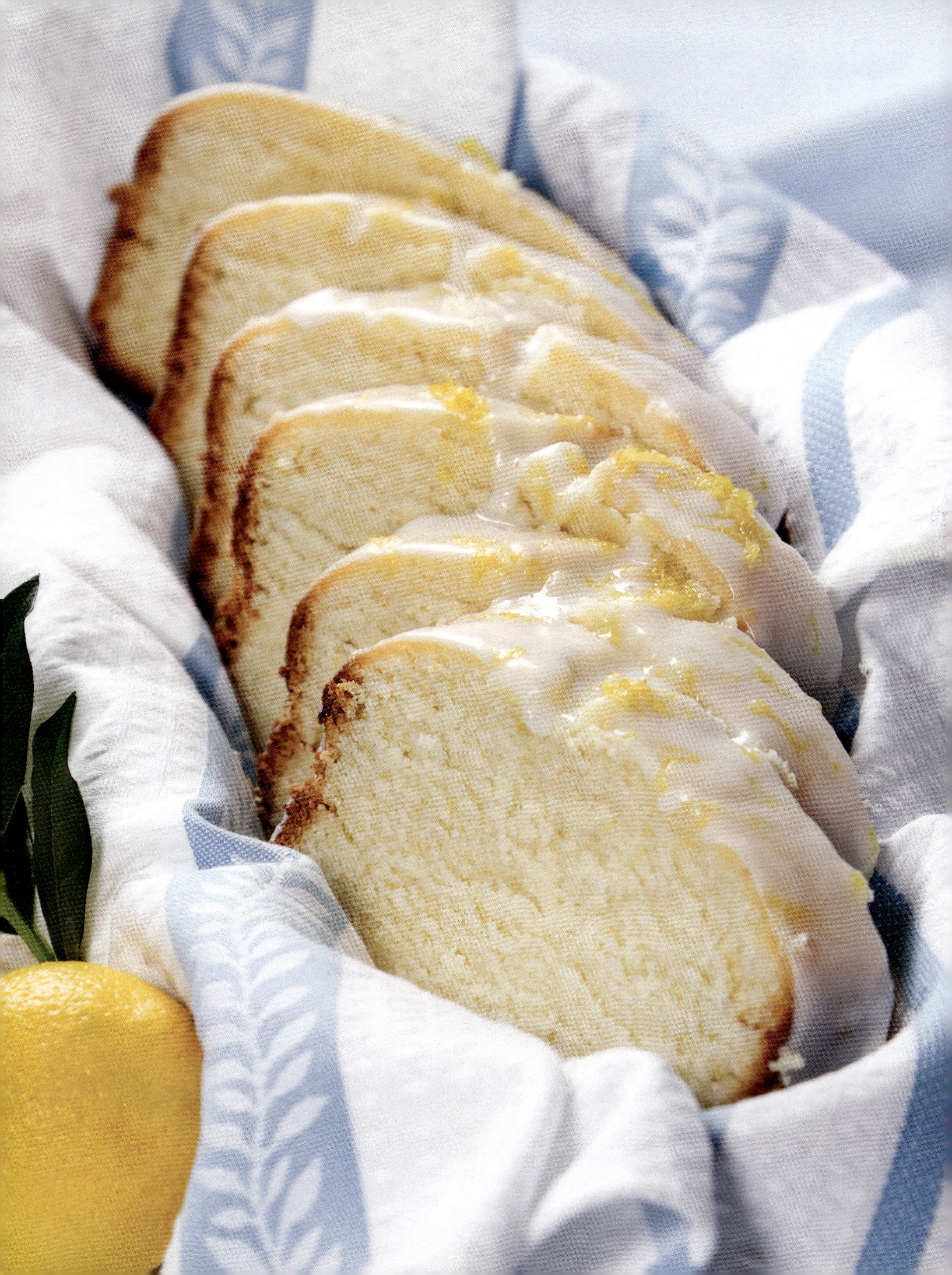

My Favorite Chocolate Pound Cake

Makes 1 loaf

Ingredients

1 cup (2 sticks) unsalted butter, softened
1¼ cups granulated sugar
4 large eggs
2 tablespoons sour cream
1 tablespoon vanilla extract

¼ cup cola or root beer
6 tablespoons good quality cocoa powder
1 teaspoon kosher salt
1¼ teaspoons baking powder
1¾ cups cake flour

Brown Butter Chocolate Frosting

2 cups powdered sugar
¼ cup brown butter (see recipe on page 57)
½ teaspoon pure vanilla extract
1/8 teaspoon kosher salt

¼ cup good quality cocoa powder
¼ cup heavy whipping cream
½ cup toasted pecans (optional)

This cake is silky in texture and contrasts well with the rich chocolaty flavor. I love this cake by itself or crowned with brown butter chocolate frosting and toasted pecans. A taste of this cake and people will be requesting the recipe. The secrets in this chocolate pound cake are the unusual addition of cola or root beer, sour cream, really good cocoa and brown butter in the frosting.

1. Place all ingredients in the order listed into the bread maker; close lid.

2. Press MENU and select CAKE.

3. Press COLOR and select DARK.

4. Press START.

5. After 5 minutes, press and hold PAUSE until machine stops; check if ingredients are uniformly mixed and use a spatula to scrape the sides; close lid and hold PAUSE to resume mixing.

6. Total machine time is 1 hour and 50 minutes.

7. In a bowl, combine frosting ingredients; mix well.

8. Spoon frosting over cooled cake, making decorative swirls with the back of the spoon.

Billowy Seven Minute Frosting

Makes 5 cups

Ingredients

2 large egg whites
2 tablespoons light corn syrup
1½ cups granulated sugar
5 tablespoons water
¼ teaspoon cream of tartar
⅛ teaspoon kosher salt
1 teaspoon pure vanilla extract
⅛ teaspoon butter vanilla extract (see source page)

This icing is like a meringue, only better. It reminds me of marshmallows, which I adore. This recipe is my favorite frosting from the Easy Moist Chocolate Cake on page 104. When I was little and living in Africa, we used to make this frosting with an old, rotary hand whisk because we did not have electricity. We would take turns cranking the handle as fast as we could and then pass it on to my mom when our arms felt like they would give out. We used to joke that the hand whisk would give us "Popeye" arms. Making it with an electric hand mixer is far easier.

1. Fashion a double boiler out of a pot containing 2 inches of water and a glass mixing bowl that will sit comfortably in the pot without touching the water.

2. Bring water in the double boiler to a simmer over medium heat.

3. In the double boiler, combine all ingredients, except vanilla and butter extract; using a hand mixer, mix on medium speed until ingredients are moistened.

4. Raise mixer speed to high and whip for 7 minutes or until mixture is very billowy and peaks form.

5. Add remaining ingredients; mix just to incorporate.

6. Use icing right away as a crust will form after 15 minutes.

Marian's Tip:
Pile this icing thickly onto the cake and swirl it into waves with the back of a spoon.

Easy Moist Chocolate Cake

Makes 1 cake

Ingredients

2 large eggs
1½ cups whole milk
⅔ cup vegetable oil
1¾ cups granulated sugar
1 teaspoon vanilla extract
½ teaspoon butter vanilla extract (see source page)
1½ teaspoons kosher salt
1 teaspoon baking powder
2 teaspoons baking soda
⅔ cup good quality cocoa powder
1⅔ cups unbleached all purpose flour

When I have a chocolate craving, I bake this cake because it is easy, moist and delicious. The secret in this cake recipe is using good quality cocoa and my favorite, butter vanilla extract.

1. Place all ingredients in the order listed into the bread maker; close lid.

2. Press MENU and select CAKE.

3. Press COLOR and select DARK.

4. Press START.

5. After 5 minutes, press and hold PAUSE until machine stops; check if ingredients are uniformly mixed and use a spatula to scrape the sides; close lid and hold PAUSE to resume mixing.

6. Total machine time is 1 hour and 50 minutes.

7. Once cake has cooled, ice the cake with billowy frosting, the recipe is on page 103.

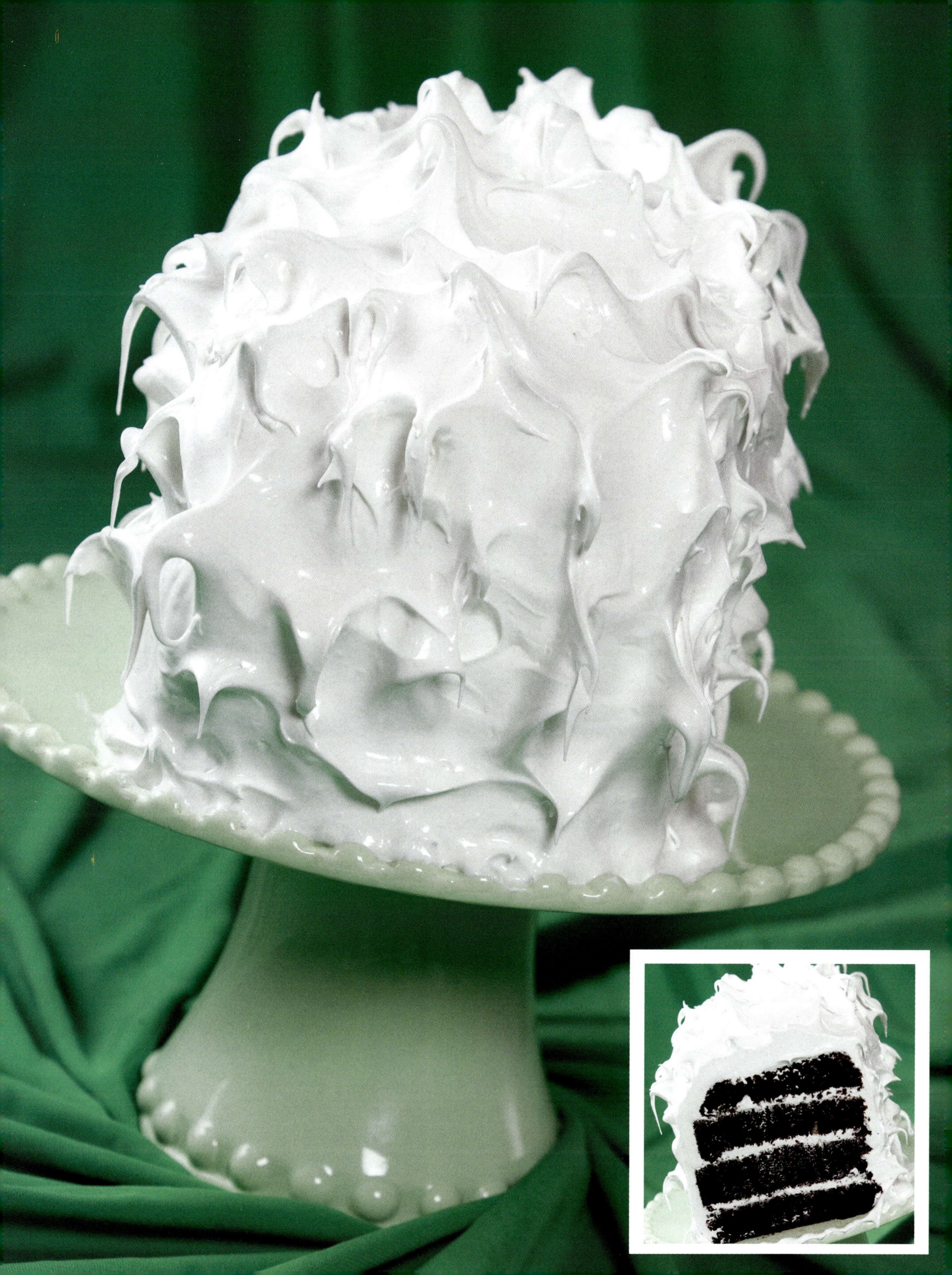

Chocolate Whipped Cream Frosting

Ingredients

1½ cups cold heavy whipping cream
½ cup powdered sugar
1 teaspoon vanilla extract
2 tablespoons good quality cocoa

This whipped cream frosting is very easy and versatile. I whip it up in just a few minutes using my immersion blender. Use good quality cocoa for this recipe.

1. In a bowl, combine all ingredients.

2. Using a hand mixer, whip on medium speed until semi stiff peaks form.

3. Spread frosting on cooled Easy Moist Chocolate Cake or serve in dollops beside still warm cake.

Glaze For Chocolate Crazy Cake

Makes 1 cup

Ingredients

¾ cup granulated sugar
¼ cup water, coconut milk or coffee
2 tablespoons cocoa powder
1 tablespoon vegetable oil
1 teaspoon pure vanilla extract
⅛ teaspoon kosher salt

This is such an easy recipe. It uses simple pantry staples and tastes so good. In addition to being a vegan glaze for the crazy cake recipe, I use it as an ice cream topping, a filling for cookies or a glaze for cream puffs.

1. Combine all ingredients in a microwave safe bowl.

2. Microwave for 4 minutes or until mixture comes to a full boil.

3. Carefully pour hot glaze over the cake and serve.

Chocolate Crazy Cake

Makes 1 cake

Ingredients

1½ cups water or coconut milk
2¼ cups unbleached all purpose flour
1¼ cups granulated sugar
4 tablespoons good quality unsweetened cocoa powder
1½ teaspoons baking soda
¾ teaspoon kosher salt
1½ teaspoons vanilla extract
⅓ cup vegetable oil
4½ teaspoons white or apple cider vinegar

Going by many other names, including Wacky Cake, and Dump Cake, this is a recipe that I grew up with. It is not only easy to make, but it is also moist and delicious. I love recipes that use simple pantry staples. It will be slightly denser and not as tall as cakes made the conventional way but the ease and hands-free way the bread maker bakes makes up for it. Top this cake with the glaze recipe on page 107. This recipe just happens to be a vegan one for people who do not consume any animal products.

1. Place all ingredients in the order listed into the bread maker; close lid.

2. Press MENU and select CAKE.

3. Press COLOR and select DARK.

4. Press START.

5. After 5 minutes, press and hold PAUSE until machine stops; check if ingredients are uniformly mixed and use a spatula to scrape the sides; close lid and hold PAUSE to resume mixing.

6. While cake is baking, prepare chocolate glaze, see recipe on page 107.

7. Total machine time is 1 hour and 50 minutes.

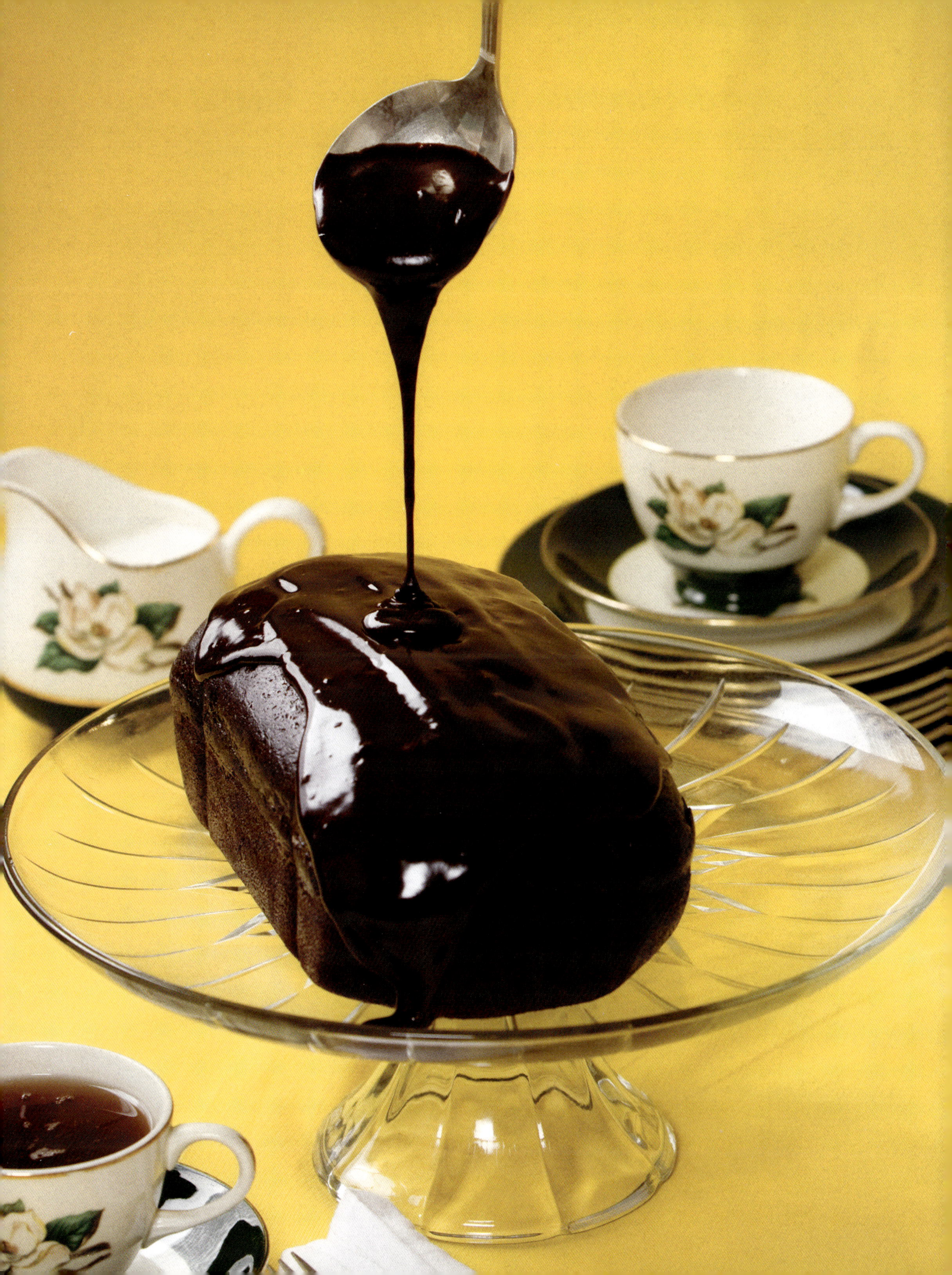

Southern Red Velvet Cake

Makes 1 cake

Ingredients

½ cup shortening

1½ cups sugar

2 eggs

2 ounces (2 bottles) red food coloring

2 tablespoons cocoa

1 teaspoon vanilla extract

2¼ cups unbleached all purpose flour, sifted

1½ teaspoons kosher salt

1 cup buttermilk

1 teaspoon baking soda

1 tablespoon white or apple cider vinegar

When Greg and I began dating in 1981, he often told me about his favorite cake. He is a Southern boy and this Red Velvet cake is his favorite cake of all time. The first time I made it, I was surprised by the strange list of ingredients. Following the recipe closely, I made this cake in my college dorm kitchen using the meagerest of tools. This cake was gorgeous and we devoured it all in one day.

1. Place all ingredients in the order listed into the bread maker; close lid.

2. Press MENU and select CAKE.

3. Press COLOR and select DARK.

4. Press START.

5. After 5 minutes, press and hold PAUSE until machine stops; check if ingredients are uniformly mixed and use a spatula to scrape the sides; close lid and hold PAUSE to resume mixing.

6. Total machine time is 2 hours.

7. Frost cooled cake with Southern Red Velvet Cake Icing (the recipe is on page 112).

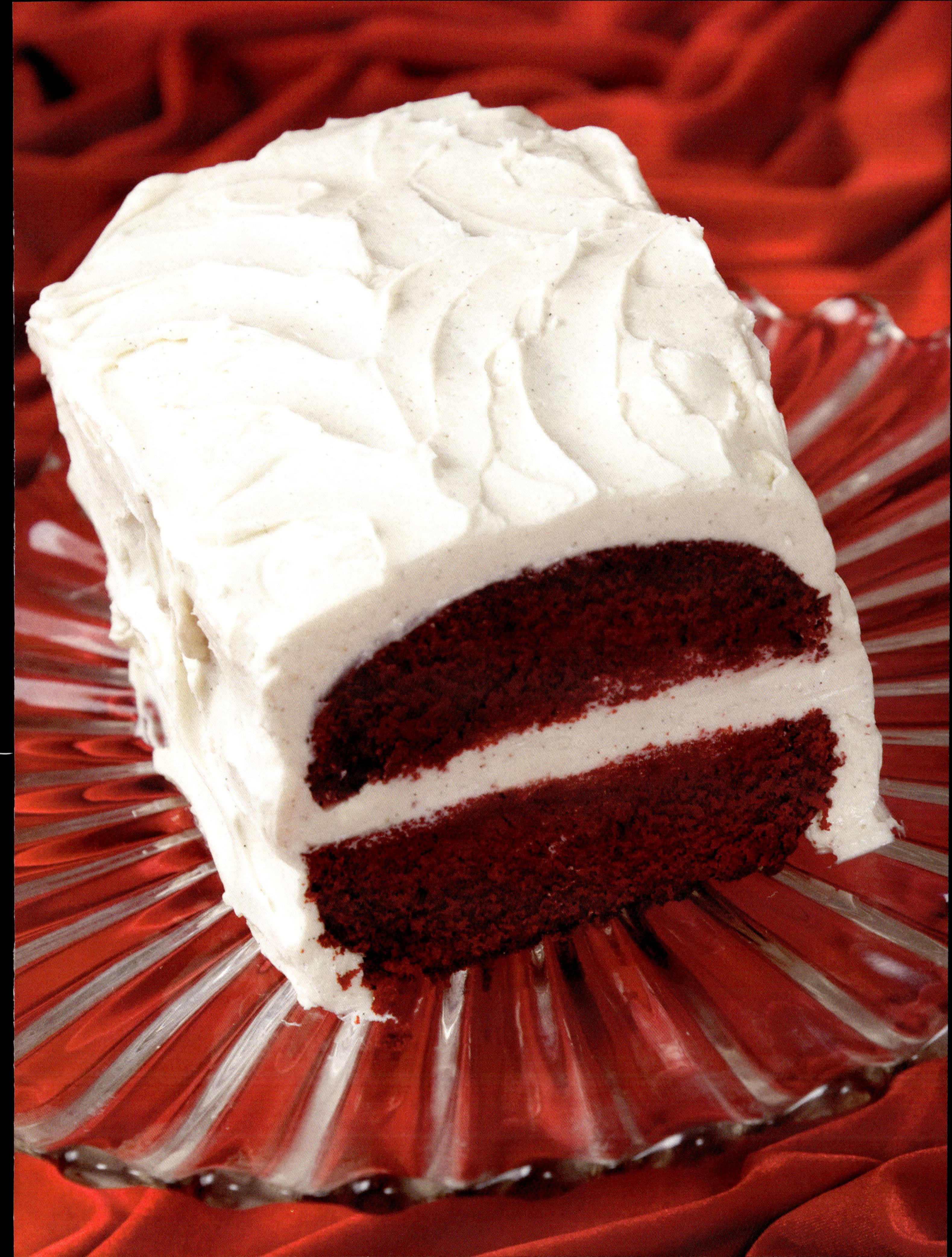

Southern Red Velvet Cake Icing

Makes 6 cups

Ingredients

2 cups whole milk
¾ cup all purpose flour
2 cups (4 sticks) unsalted butter, softened
2 cups granulated sugar
2 teaspoons pure vanilla extract

This is such an amazing recipe! It starts off looking like a recipe for white or cream gravy. In fact, old recipes for this icing call it "gravy icing". Once this strange, gravy paste gets whipped into butter and sugar, the most wonderful transformation takes place. It is so fluffy and has the most subtle, soft flavor that is completely addicting. Some people prefer cream cheese icing on Red Velvet Cake. I think that's only because they have never tried this recipe.

1. In a saucepan over medium heat, combine milk and flour; whisk until mixture thickens and is rapidly bubbling.

2. Remove from heat and cover with plastic wrap; chill.

3. Using a hand or stand mixer, cream butter and sugar for 5 minutes or until fluffy.

4. Add vanilla to the mixture; mix for an additional 1 minute.

5. Combine flour mixture with sugar mixture; mix on high speed for 3-7 minutes or until icing is billowy and you can't feel any sugar grains on your tongue when tasting.

6. Fill and frost cake with icing.

Gluten-Free Recipes

My Favorite Gluten-Free Bread	114
Gluten-Free Garlic Herb Bread	116
Gluten-Free Rice Bread	118
Gluten-Free Pizza Dough	120
Gluten-Free Buttercrust Bread	122
Gluten-Free Stuffing Bread	123
Gluten-Free Corn Bread	124
Gluten-Free Banana Bread	126
Gluten-Free Zucchini Bread	128
Brown Butter Chocolate Frosting	129
Gluten-Free Chocolate Pound Cake	130
Gluten-Free Brownies	132

My Favorite Gluten-Free Bread

Makes 1 loaf

Ingredients

⅓ cup buttermilk
4 large eggs
⅔ cup water
¼ cup brown butter (see recipe on page 57)
1 teaspoon apple cider vinegar
2 tablespoons tamari
3 tablespoons honey
1 cup tapioca flour
1 cup corn starch
⅓ cup almond flour, toasted

¾ cup garfava flour (a mixture of garbanzo bean and fava bean flour)
¼ cup sorghum flour
2 tablespoons flax seed meal
3 tablespoons powdered milk
1 tablespoon kosher salt
1 tablespoon unflavored gelatin
1 tablespoon xanthan gum
1 tablespoon bread machine yeast

I have fallen in love with making gluten-free breads. It is a challenge to try to create breads that are as close as possible to their wheat-based counter parts but I enjoy the challenge. I really like this recipe. It is light and springy with lovely flecks from the almond meal. If you are new to gluten-free baking, please see the source page for locations where you can purchase some of these wondrously strange ingredients. Also, please refer to the bread making tips section in the front of the book to see what all of these ingredients contribute to the finished loaf.

1. Place buttermilk, eggs, water, brown butter, vinegar, tamari and honey into bread maker.

2. In a bowl, combine remaining ingredients; mix well using a hand whisk and pour it into the bread maker.

3. Close lid.

4. Press MENU and select GLUTEN FREE.

5. Press COLOR and select DARK.

6. Press START.

7. Total machine time is 2 hours and 50 minutes.

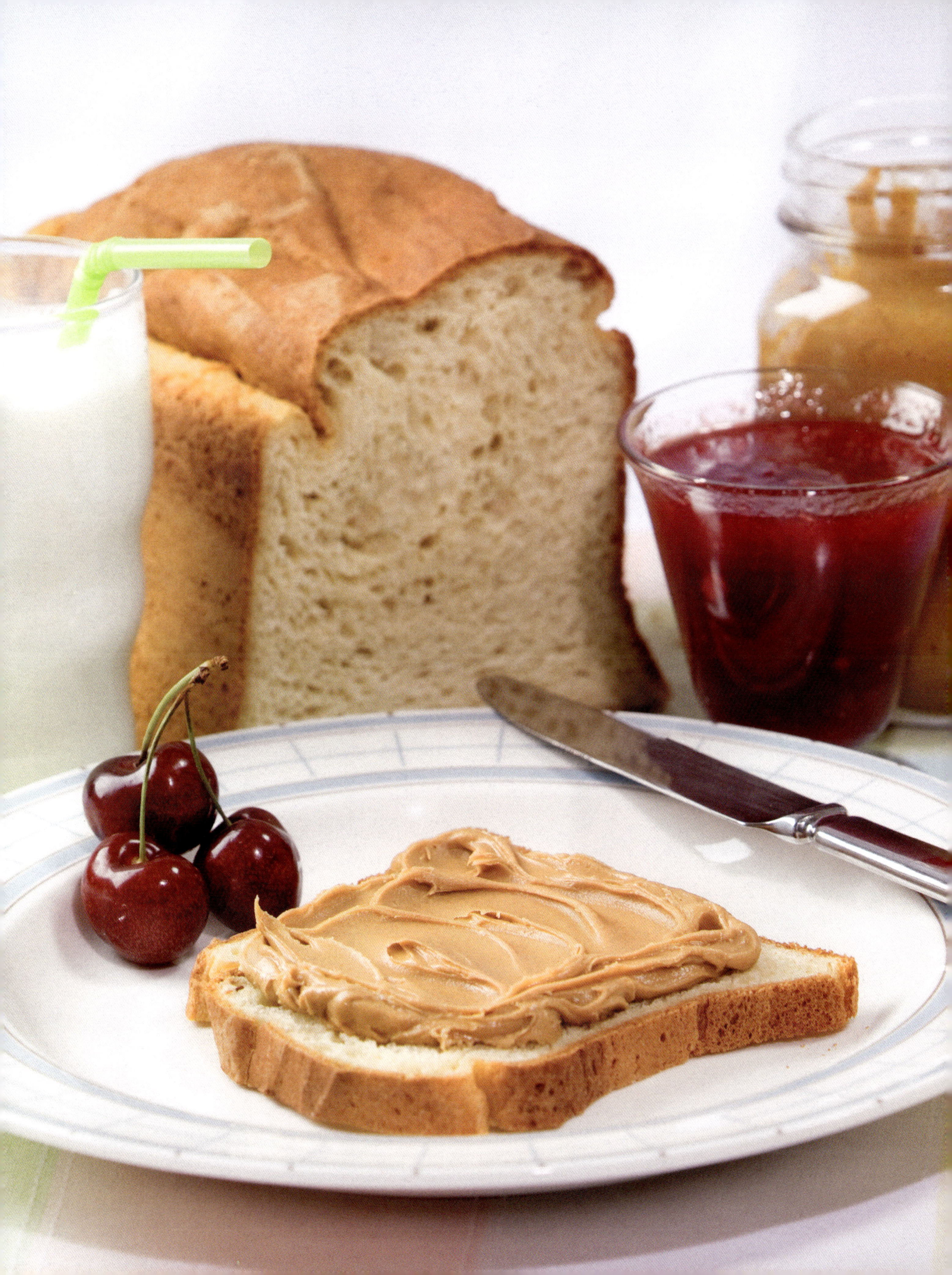

Gluten-Free Garlic Herb Bread

Makes 1 loaf

Ingredients

1 cup + 2 tablespoons water
¼ cup olive oil
1 teaspoon apple cider vinegar
3 large eggs
1 tablespoon tamari
6 garlic cloves, chopped
¼ cup yellow onion, chopped
1 tablespoon fresh rosemary, chopped
2 teaspoons fresh thyme, chopped
10-12 fresh basil leaves, torn
1 tablespoon kosher salt

2 cups brown rice flour
⅓ cup potato starch flour
⅓ cup tapioca starch flour
⅓ cup garfava flour (a mixture of garbanzo bean and fava bean flour)
2 tablespoons powdered egg whites
¼ cup granulated sugar
2 teaspoons xanthan gum
2 teaspoons unflavored gelatin
2½ teaspoons bread machine yeast

This bread is a nice change for those who cannot eat gluten, especially those who are accustomed to buying gluten-free breads in a store. This recipe is great with a bowl of soup, as hearty sandwiches or with just a drizzle of good olive oil. The flavors are really big and bold, making this recipe a real treat for the taste buds.

1. Place water, oil, vinegar, eggs, tamari, garlic, onions, rosemary, thyme and basil into the bread maker.

2. In a bowl, combine remaining ingredients; whisk very well.

3. Pour mixture into the bread maker; close lid.

4. Press MENU and select GLUTEN FREE.

5. Press COLOR and select DARK.

6. Press START.

7. Total machine time 2 hours and 50 minutes.

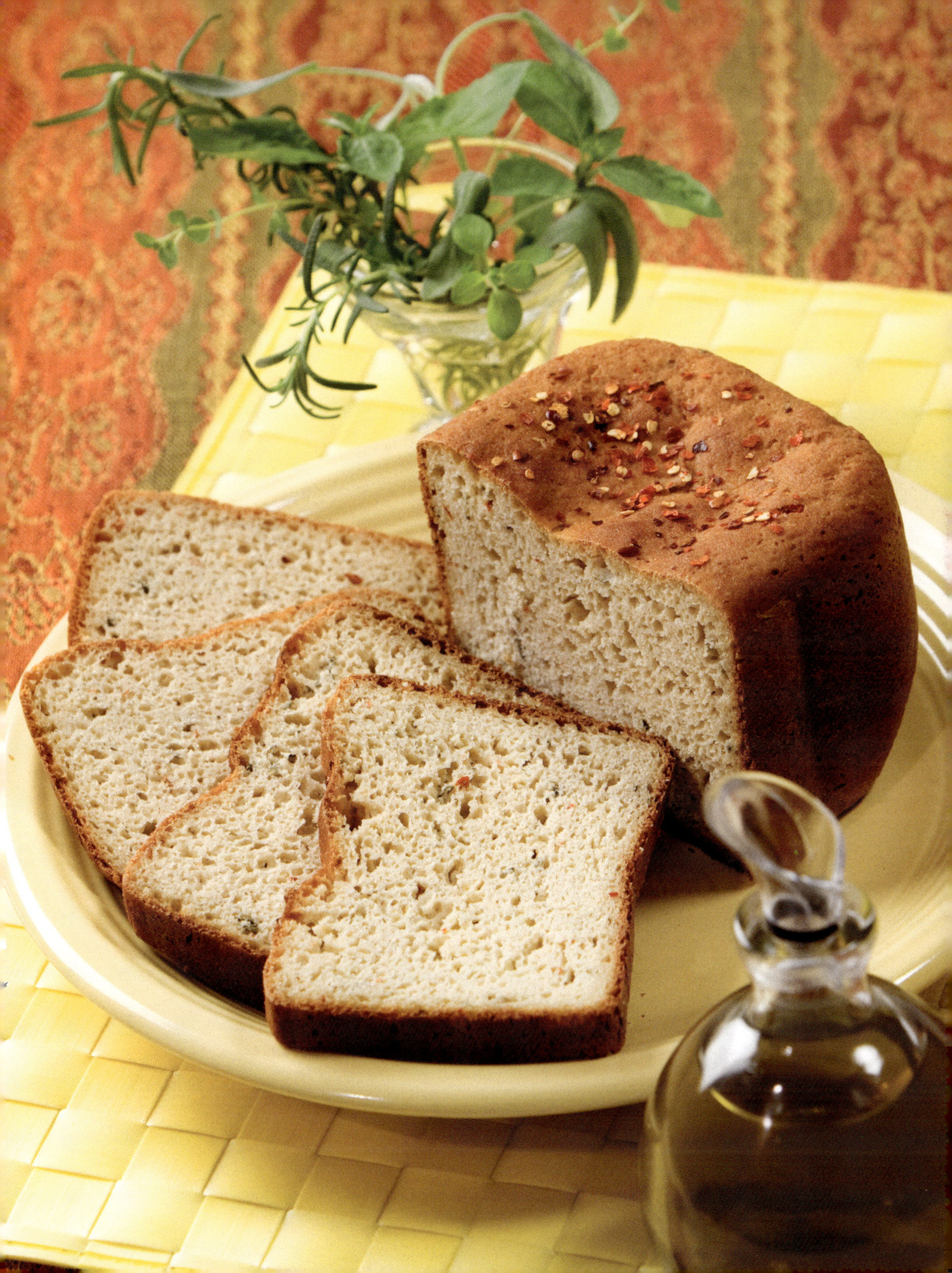

Gluten-Free Rice Bread

Makes 1 loaf

Ingredients

1 cup + 2 tablespoons water
¼ cup unsalted butter, softened
1 cup brown rice flour
1 cup cornstarch
½ cup garfava flour (a mixture of garbanzo bean and fava bean flour)
½ cup tapioca flour
1 tablespoon kosher salt
2 tablespoons powdered egg whites
1 tablespoon unflavored gelatin
1 tablespoon xanthan gum
3 tablespoons powdered milk
1 tablespoon bread machine yeast
2 tablespoons granulated sugar
1 teaspoon apple cider vinegar

I have come to love gluten-free baking. The breads are the most challenging to make because it is hard to replicate the magic gluten gives a regular loaf of yeast bread. Since gluten causes such misery and danger in people who cannot consume it, the answer is to create the very best bread possible, full of flavor and interesting texture, which is what this bread is all about.

1. Place water and butter into the bread maker.

2. In a bowl, combine remaining ingredients; mix very well using a hand whisk.

3. Pour mixture into the bread maker; close lid.

4. Press MENU and select GLUTEN FREE.

5. Press COLOR and select DARK.

6. Press START.

7. Total machine time 2 hours and 50 minutes.

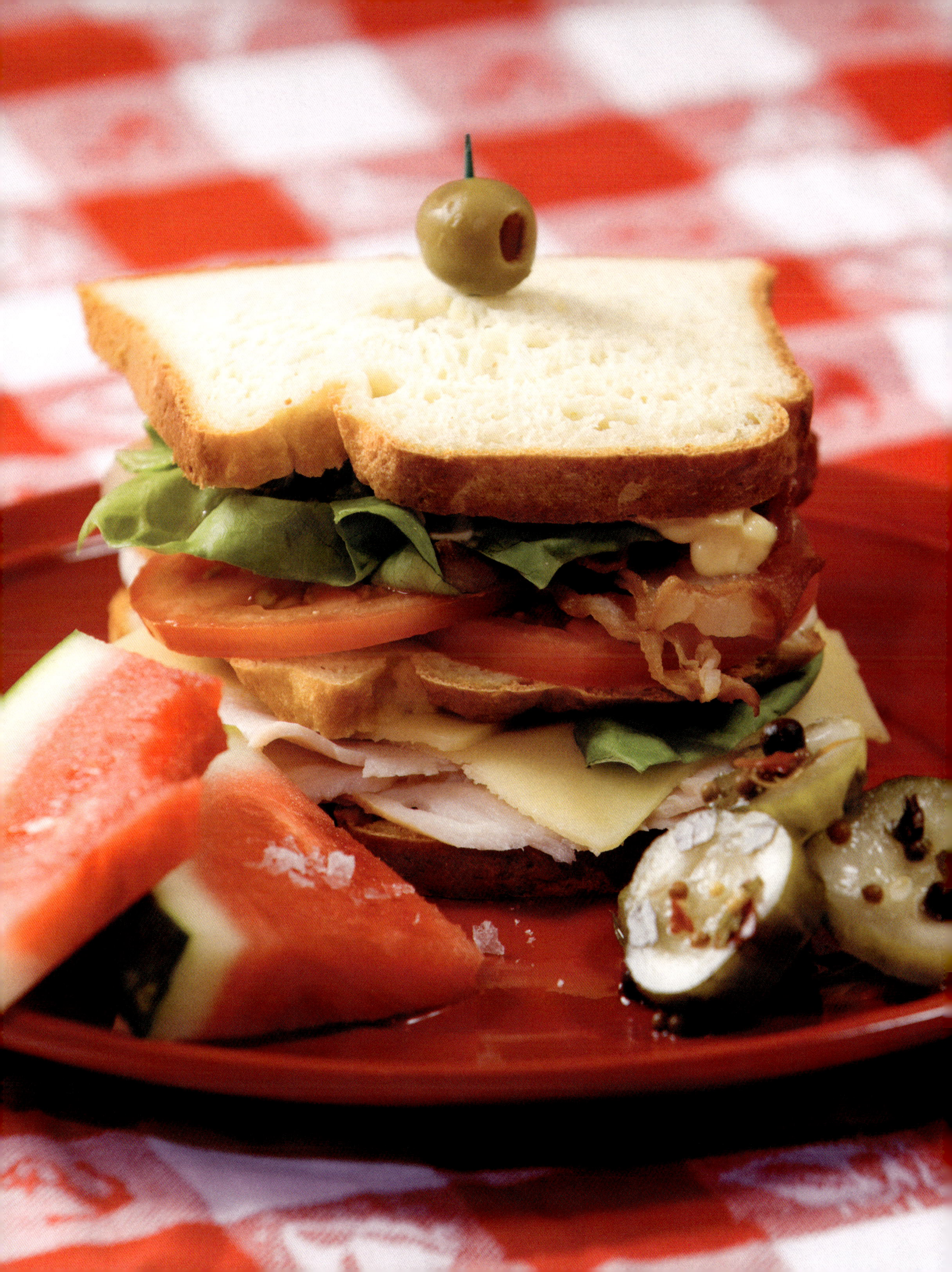

Gluten-Free Pizza Dough

Makes 2 pizzas

Ingredients

2 tablespoons brown butter (see recipe on page 57)
1 cup + 2 tablespoons water
1/3 cup dry potato flakes
1 cup white rice flour
1/2 cup tapioca flour
3 tablespoons powdered milk
1 teaspoon onion powder

1 teaspoon kosher salt
2 teaspoons xanthan gum
2 teaspoons unflavored gelatin
1 tablespoon bread machine yeast
3 tablespoons dried egg whites
1 tablespoon granulated sugar

I developed this recipe for my brother-in-law, Sam, who is allergic to gluten and wheat. When he tasted this crust, he was so happy. Not having enjoyed pizza in many years, Sam exclaimed, "This is killer!" In the past, he tried a few store bought mixes and prepared crusts but they were all rather tasteless and crumbly. This one is full of flavor, crunchy and is thoroughly enjoyed by everyone. The bread machine has both a GLUTEN FREE setting and a DOUGH setting. For this recipe, you will use the DOUGH setting and then finish baking the pizza in the oven. I like to make a double batch and freeze the dough balls for later enjoyment.

1. Place brown butter and water into the bread maker.

2. In a bowl, combine remaining ingredients; mix well using a hand whisk, pour into bread maker and close the lid.

3. Press MENU and select DOUGH.

4. Press START.

5. Total machine time is 1 hour and 30 minutes.

6. When cycle is complete, divide dough into two dough balls.

7. To make a pizza, pat out the dough on an oiled baking sheet and let rest for 20 minutes. Bake without toppings at 425 degrees for 15-18 minutes. Add desired toppings and bake for an additional 12-15 minutes.

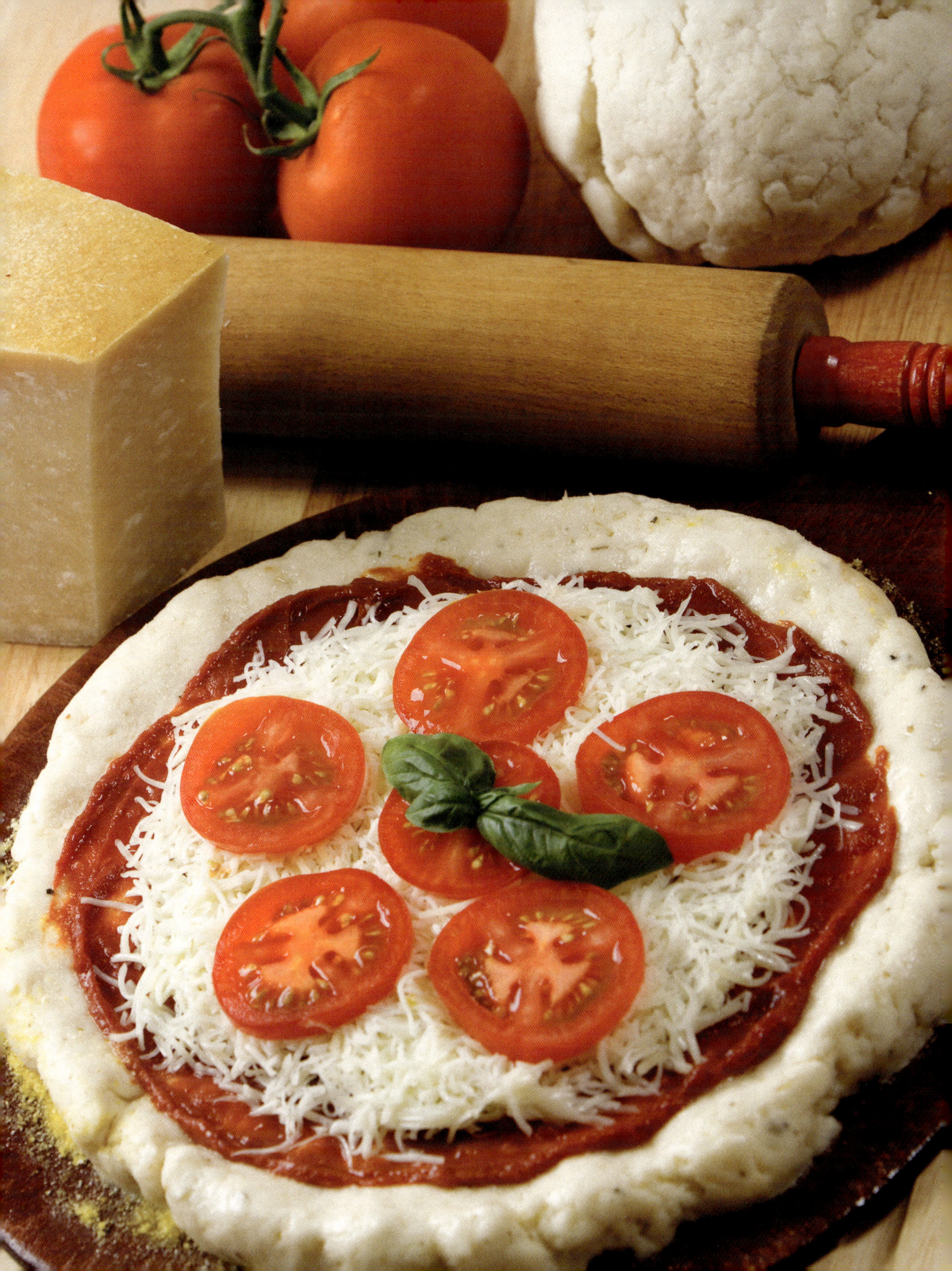

Gluten-Free Buttercrust Bread

Makes 1 loaf

Ingredients

1½ cups water
1 teaspoon apple cider vinegar
5 tablespoons unsalted butter, softened
3 large eggs
6 tablespoons powdered milk
3 tablespoons granulated sugar
1 cup corn starch
¾ cup garfava flour (a mixture of garbanzo bean and fava bean flours)
¼ cup sorghum flour
1 cup tapioca starch flour
1 tablespoon xanthan gum
1 tablespoon unflavored gelatin
1 tablespoon kosher salt
1 tablespoon + 1 teaspoon bread machine yeast

It has been an adventure coming up with recipes that my brother-in-law Sam can enjoy. The texture of gluten-free bread is different from breads that contain gluten, but the flavors are wonderful. Before baking, the batter is very thick. The xanthan gum and gelatin help to provide chewiness and some spring. The eggs and milk powder add protein and improve the texture. It is normal for gluten-free loaves to be sort of flat on top.

1. Place water, apple cider vinegar, butter and eggs into the bread maker.

2. In a bowl, combine remaining ingredients; mix well using a hand whisk and pour into bread maker.

3. Close lid.

4. Press MENU and select GLUTEN FREE.

5. Press COLOR and select DARK.

6. Press START.

7. Total machine time is 2 hours and 50 minutes.

Gluten-Free Stuffing Bread

Makes 1 loaf

Ingredients

1¾ cups water
5 tablespoons brown butter (see recipe on page 57)
1 teaspoon apple cider vinegar
3 large egg whites
1 celery rib, finely diced
1 carrot, finely diced
½ medium yellow onion, finely diced
1 tablespoon fresh sage, chopped
1 cup tapioca flour

1 cup corn starch
¾ cup garfava flour (a mixture of garbanzo bean and fava bean flours)
¼ cup sorghum flour
1 tablespoon kosher salt
1 tablespoon brown sugar
2 teaspoons xanthan gum
2 teaspoons unflavored gelatin
1 tablespoon bread machine yeast

I created this recipe to turn bread into stuffing for our holiday turkey. Although my brother-in-law is allergic to gluten and wheat, I wanted to make his favorite "pre-allergy" stuffing recipe. This bread is the happy result. We like it so much that we make it in loaf form as well as for stuffing. It makes fantastic turkey sandwiches and pairs well with roast pork or chicken. While the texture is different from wheat breads, the flavor is superb.

1. Place water, brown butter, vinegar, egg whites, celery, carrots, onions and sage into bread maker.

2. In a bowl, combine remaining ingredients; mix well using a hand whisk, pour into bread maker and close lid.

3. Press MENU and select GLUTEN FREE.

4. Press COLOR and select DARK.

5. Press START.

6. Total machine time is 2 hours and 50 minutes.

Gluten-Free Corn Bread

Makes 1 loaf

Ingredients

1 large egg
1¼ cups buttermilk
½ cup (1 stick) unsalted butter, softened
½ cup corn
1 cup masa harina (corn flour used in corn tortillas)
½ cup sweet rice flour
½ cup potato starch flour

2 teaspoons xanthan gum
1 teaspoon baking soda
½ teaspoon baking powder
2 teaspoons kosher salt
2 tablespoons grits, uncooked
¼ cup granulated sugar

Corn bread is a treat for everyone, especially for those who can't tolerate gluten. This is also a treat for anyone who just loves good, moist corn bread. This corn bread is on the sweeter side but you can easily omit the sugar without making the recipe suffer. This loaf is very tender and a bit shaggy when sliced, thanks to the whole kernel corn in it. I love to serve this with honey butter on the side. It is satisfying enough that you won't need a dessert.

1. Place egg, buttermilk, butter and corn into bread maker.

2. In a bowl, combine remaining ingredients; mix well using a hand whisk and pour into bread maker.

3. Close lid.

4. Press MENU and select GLUTEN FREE.

5. Press COLOR and select DARK.

6. Press START.

7. Total machine time is 2 hours and 50 minutes.

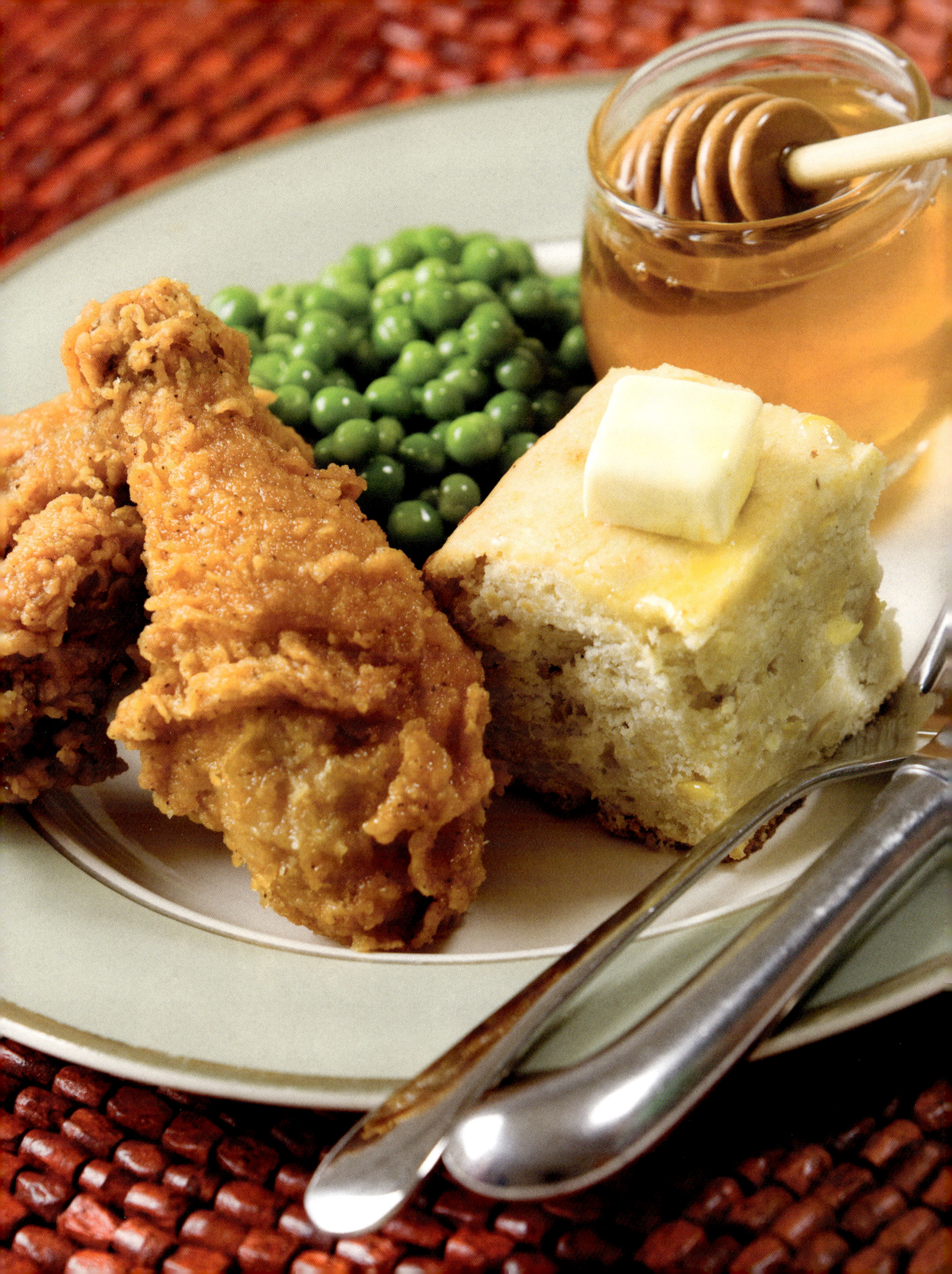

Gluten-Free Banana Bread

Makes 1 loaf

Ingredients

½ cup (1 stick) unsalted butter, softened
2 large eggs
4 large overripe bananas, sliced
3 tablespoons sour cream
1 teaspoon vanilla
1 cup granulated sugar
1 teaspoon baking soda
½ teaspoon baking powder

1 teaspoon kosher salt
½ cup cornstarch
1 cup brown rice flour
½ cup potato starch flour
½ cup tapioca flour
2 tablespoons powdered egg whites
2 teaspoons xanthan gum
2 teaspoons unflavored gelatin

Since one of my favorite foods is banana bread, I was very happy to adapt this childhood recipe for a gluten-free lifestyle. The ingredient list for gluten-free baked goods is always a long one, but at least the bread maker makes the rest easy. Simply measure the ingredients and dump them in to enjoy a really delicious and moist banana bread.

1. Place butter, eggs, bananas, sour cream and vanilla into the bread maker.

2. In a bowl, combine remaining ingredients; whisk very well.

3. Pour mixture into the bread maker; close lid.

4. Press MENU and select QUICK.

5. Press COLOR and select DARK.

6. Press START.

7. After 5 minutes, press and hold PAUSE until machine stops; check if ingredients are uniformly mixed and use a spatula to scrape the sides; close lid and hold PAUSE to resume mixing.

8. Total machine time is 2 hours and 10 minutes.

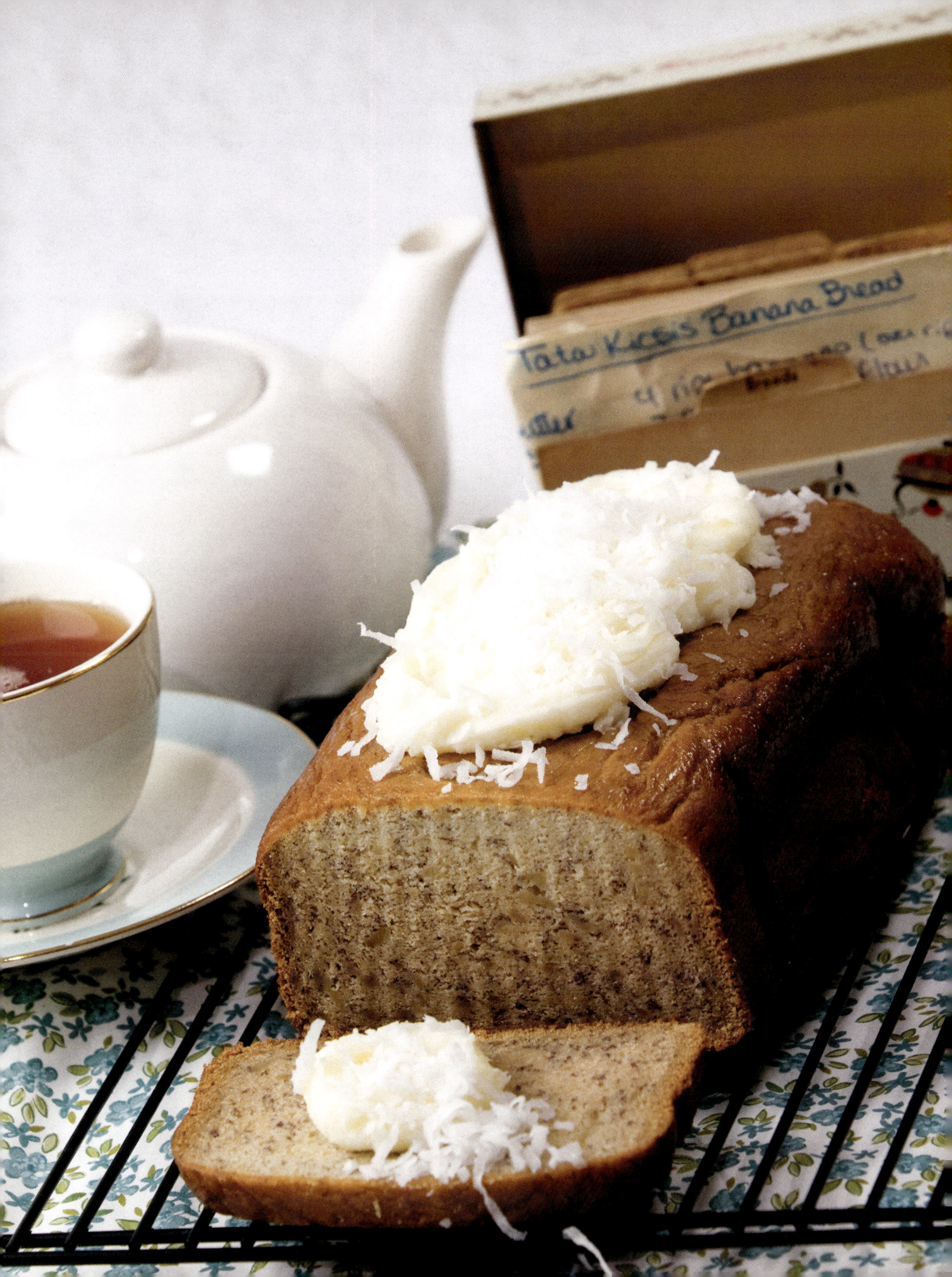
Banana Bread

Gluten-Free Zucchini Bread

Makes 1 loaf

Ingredients

3 cups zucchini, shredded
1½ cups granulated sugar
6 tablespoons unsalted butter, softened
2 large eggs
¼ cup sour cream
1 tablespoon lemon juice
½ cup sweet rice flour
¾ cup tapioca flour
¾ cup cornstarch

1 tablespoon potato flour
1 teaspoon unflavored gelatin
1 teaspoon xanthan gum
1 teaspoon baking soda
1 teaspoon baking powder
¼ teaspoon ground cinnamon
1¼ teaspoons kosher salt
½ cup pecan pieces

Zucchini adds the perfect moisture to this delicious recipe. It keeps well and freezes beautifully. Each time I make a batch, I hope to have some of it leftover for breakfast the next day. It's so delicious that it never seems to make it that long.

1. Place zucchini on a kitchen towel and squeeze to remove as much water as possible.

2. Place zucchini, sugar, butter, eggs, sour cream and lemon juice into bread maker.

3. In a bowl, combine remaining ingredients; mix well using a hand whisk, pour into bread maker and close lid.

4. Press MENU and select QUICK.

5. Press COLOR and select DARK.

6. Press START.

7. After 5 minutes, press and hold PAUSE until machine stops; check if ingredients are uniformly mixed and use a spatula to scrape the sides; close lid and hold PAUSE to resume mixing.

8. Total machine time is 2 hours and 10 minutes.

Brown Butter Chocolate Frosting

Makes 2 cups

Ingredients

2 cups powdered sugar
¼ cup brown butter (see recipe on page 57)
½ teaspoon pure vanilla extract
⅛ teaspoon kosher salt
¼ cup good quality cocoa powder
¼ cup heavy whipping cream

Brown butter as an ingredient in any recipe adds a very distinct flavor. This is especially true for this frosting recipe. The combination of brown butter and a good quality cocoa is truly amazing.

1. In a bowl, combine all ingredients; stir with a spoon.

2. Spoon over cooled Gluten-Free Chocolate Pound Cake.

3. Make decorative swirls using the back of the spoon.

Gluten-Free Chocolate Pound Cake

Makes 1 cake

Ingredients

1 cup unsalted butter, softened
1¼ cups granulated sugar
4 large eggs
2 tablespoons sour cream
1 tablespoon vanilla extract
¼ cup cola or root beer
6 tablespoons good quality cocoa powder
1 teaspoon kosher salt

1¼ teaspoons baking powder
½ cup sweet rice flour
½ cup tapioca flour
¾ cup cornstarch
1 tablespoon potato flour
1 teaspoon unflavored gelatin
1 teaspoon xanthan gum

I have found that it is quite easy to convert recipes containing wheat flour into excellent gluten-free versions. This is certainly the case in this cake recipe. The list of ingredients in gluten-free baking is always a long one, but I have come to love those wondrously strange ingredients. Creating something delicious without the use of wheat flour, which may be dangerous to those allergic to it, is something I never get tired of.

1. Place butter, sugar, eggs, sour cream, vanilla, cola, cocoa powder, salt and baking powder into the bread maker.

2. In a bowl, combine remaining ingredients and whisk very well using a hand whisk; pour mixture into the bread maker and close the lid.

3. Press MENU and select CAKE.

4. Press COLOR and select DARK.

5. Press START.

6. After 5 minutes, press and hold PAUSE until machine stops; check if ingredients are uniformly mixed and use a spatula to scrape the sides; close lid and hold PAUSE to resume mixing.

7. Total machine time is 1 hour and 50 minutes.

8. Once cake has completely cooled, frost it with my Brown Butter Chocolate Frosting (the recipe is on page 129).

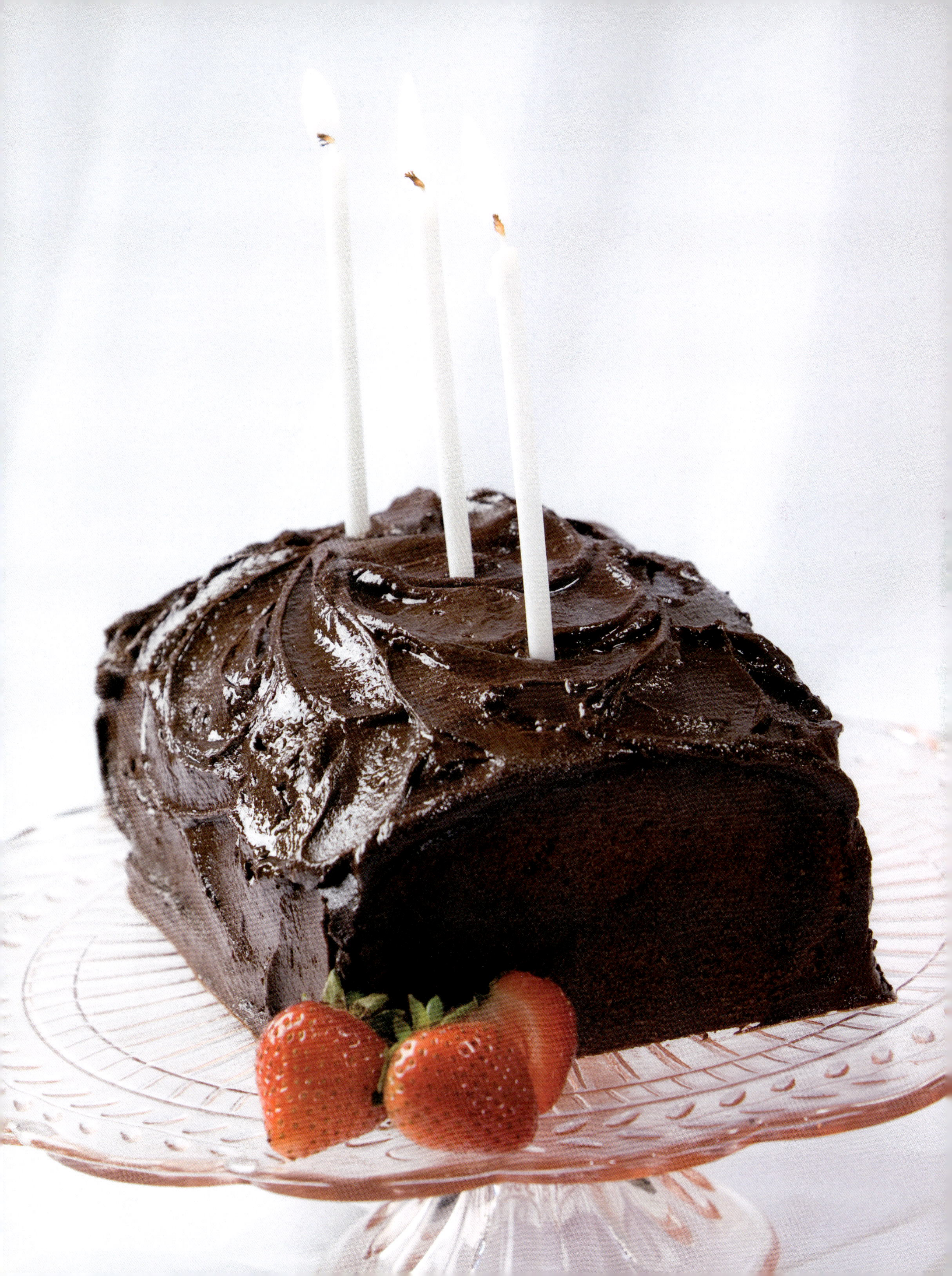

Gluten-Free Brownies

Makes 12-16 brownies

Ingredients

1 cup unsalted butter, softened
2 cups granulated sugar
4 large eggs
¼ teaspoon kosher salt
1 teaspoon vanilla extract
½ cup high quality cocoa

¼ cup sweet rice flour
⅓ cup tapioca flour
⅓ cup cornstarch
2 teaspoons potato flour
½ teaspoon unflavored gelatin
½ teaspoon xanthan gum

After trying brownie recipes from many gluten-free cookbooks, I finally figured out that the best way to make an excellent tasting brownie is to use recipes I already love and adapt them using gluten-free ingredients. This gluten-free version is so excellent that I can't tell it apart from the original. The bread maker is perfect at making brownies that are a bit chewy around the edges while still soft and fudgy in the middle.

1. Place butter, sugar, eggs, salt and vanilla extract into bread maker.

2. In a bowl, combine remaining ingredients; mix well using a hand whisk and pour into bread maker.

3. Close lid.

4. Press MENU and select CAKE.

5. Press COLOR and select DARK.

6. Press START.

7. After 5 minutes, press and hold PAUSE until machine stops; check if ingredients are uniformly mixed and use a spatula to scrape the sides; close lid and hold PAUSE to resume mixing.

8. Total machine time is 1 hour and 50 minutes.

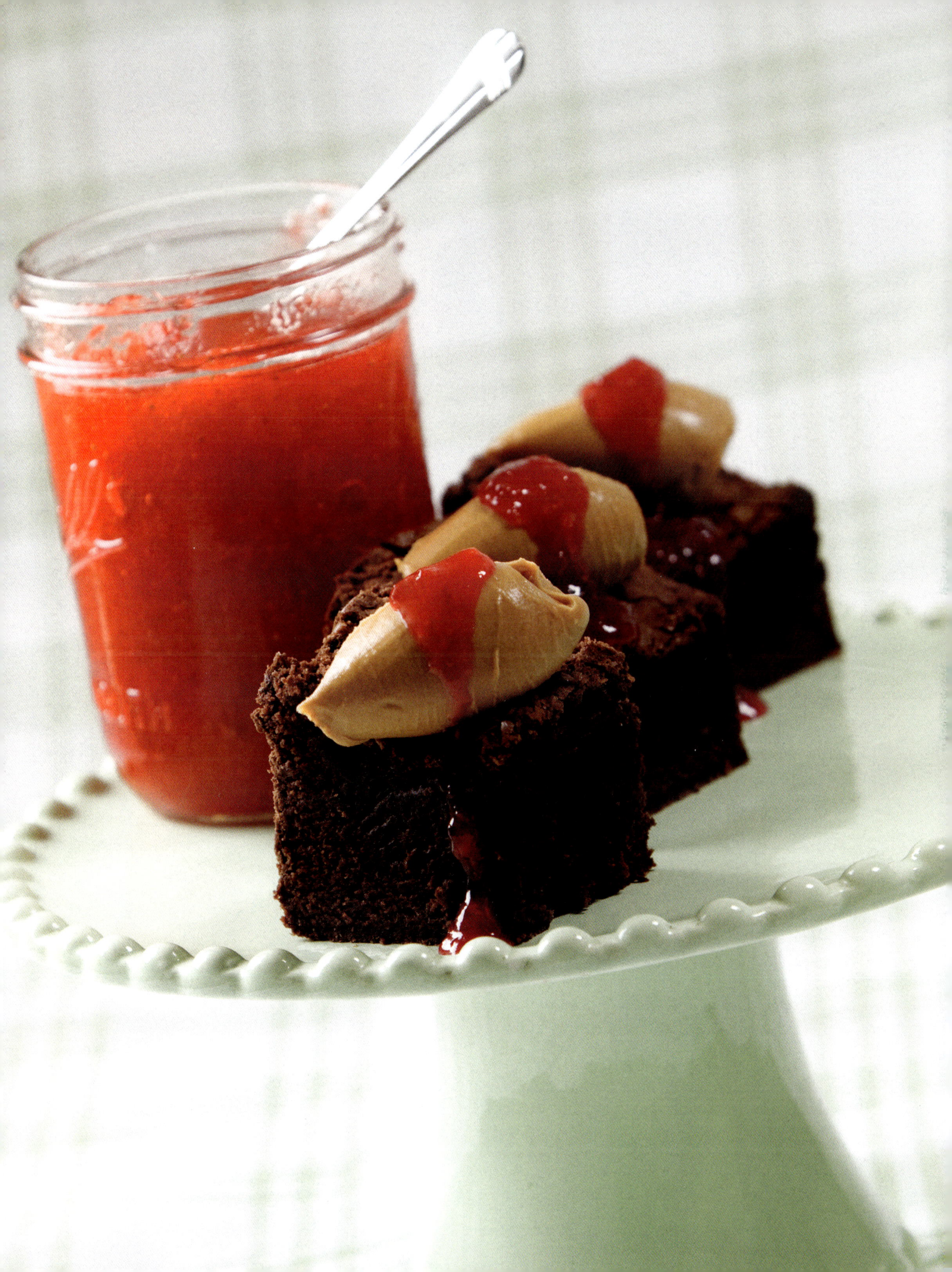

Jams, Jellies & More

Easy Anytime Apple Butter	135
Homemade Strawberry Jelly	136
Greg's Favorite Blueberry Jam	138
Michigan Tart Red Cherry Jam	140
Pretty Peach Preserves	142
Harvest Pear Jam	144
Pretty Plum Preserves	146
Florida Tangerine Maralade	148
Kiwi Jam	150
Lemon Curd	152
Hot Red Pepper Jelly	154
Mango Chutney	155
Rhubarb Jam	156

Easy Anytime Apple Butter

Makes 4 cups

Ingredients

4 apples, cored, unpeeled and pureed
1 cup packed light brown sugar
1 tablespoon fresh lemon juice
1 tablespoon ground cinnamon
1 teaspoon ground clove
½ teaspoon ground nutmeg
½ teaspoon ground allspice

Although I have made apple butter on the stove top many times, I have often scorched it. Unless you stir it constantly, it can be tricky to make because it thickens as it cooks and scorches or burns easily. The bread maker's JAM setting is perfect for making this recipe the easy, hands-free way. The bread maker stirs it just right and the results are always great. I like to use a variety of apples. My favorites are Granny Smith, Golden Delicious, Pink Lady and Northern Spy.

1. Place apples into a blender; mix until smooth.
2. Place apples and remaining ingredients into the bread maker; close lid.
3. Press MENU and select JAM.
4. Press START.
5. Total machine time is 1 hour and 20 minutes.

Homemade Strawberry Jelly

Makes 4 cups

Ingredients

2 cups fresh strawberry pulp from 1 pound of strawberries, hulled and crushed
3½ cups granulated sugar
1 pouch (3 ounces) liquid fruit pectin
½ teaspoon citric acid

If you have never made homemade jam from scratch before, try this recipe. It is important to measure accurately when making jams or jellies. Citric acid is added to this recipe in place of lemon juice because it adds a delightful tartness, without adding a flavor of its own. The citric acid, when combined with the pectin, is what causes the jam to thicken. This jam is a great gift. No one needs to know that it is utter child's play to make.

1. Place all ingredients in the order listed into the bread maker; stir until sugar is moistened and close the lid.

2. Press MENU and select JAM.

3. Press START (unit will heat for 15 minutes before paddles start turning).

4. Total machine time is 1 hour and 20 minutes.

Marian's Fresh Strawberry Jelly
Marian's Fresh Strawberry Jelly
4 CUPS

Greg's Favorite Blueberry Jam

Makes 4 cups

Ingredients

2 cups fresh blueberry puree, from 2 pints of fresh blueberries
½ teaspoon citric acid
3½ cups granulated sugar
1 pouch (3 ounces) liquid fruit pectin

We love to go blueberry picking in the summer. Since this is Greg's favorite jam, he is always eager to go berry picking. I think we enjoy each other's company as much as we enjoy picking fragrant, plump berries and dreaming of all the wonderful ways to make desserts with them. I always start with fresh blueberry shortcake. That way, the berries can be enjoyed in their perfect, uncooked state. I then make blueberry ice cream, cobblers, pies and of course, this jam. Since it is often unavailable in grocery stores, blueberry jam makes an especially thoughtful gift.

1. Place all ingredients in the order listed into the bread maker; stir until sugar is moistened and close the lid.

2. Press MENU and select JAM.

3. Press START (unit will heat for 15 minutes before paddles start turning).

4. Total machine time is 1 hour and 20 minutes.

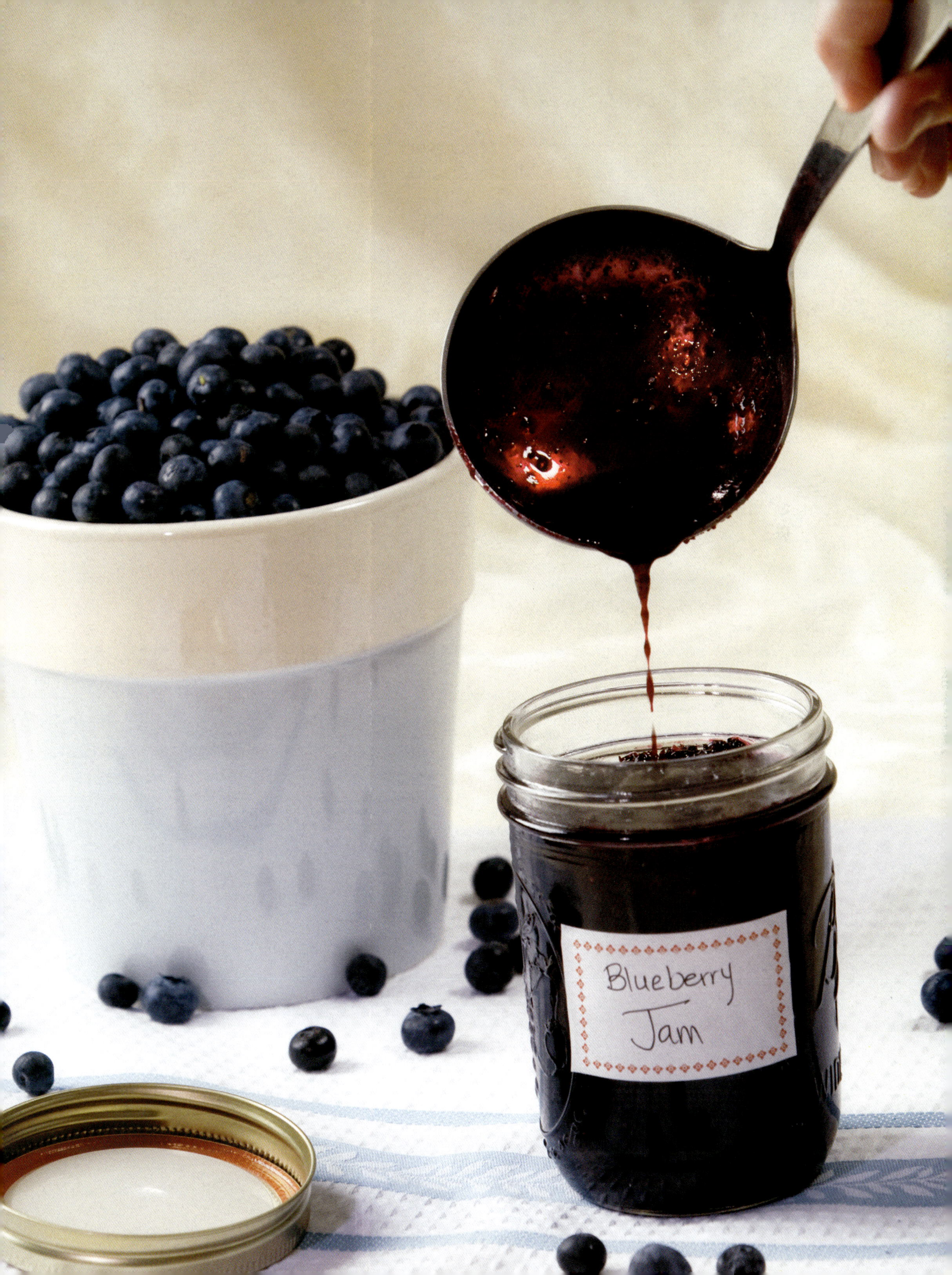
Blueberry
Jam

Michigan Tart Red Cherry Jam

Makes 4 cups

Ingredients

2 cups tart red cherries, pitted and finely chopped
3 1/8 cups granulated sugar
1 pouch (3 ounces) liquid fruit pectin
1/4 teaspoon citric acid

I was born in the tiny town of Greenville, Michigan. My dad is from the even tinier town of Belding, Michigan. The annual crops of tart red cherries grown in Michigan (where 75% of our nation's yearly crop is grown) are truly wonderful in every way. The cherries are bright red and just tart enough to make perfect baked goods and preserves. This jam is one of my preferred ways to showcase their delicious charm.

1. Place all ingredients in the order listed into the bread maker; stir until sugar is moistened and close the lid.

2. Press MENU and select JAM.

3. Press START (unit will heat for 15 minutes before paddles start turning).

4. Total machine time is 1 hour and 20 minutes.

Marian's Tip:
This is a great filling for jelly donuts.

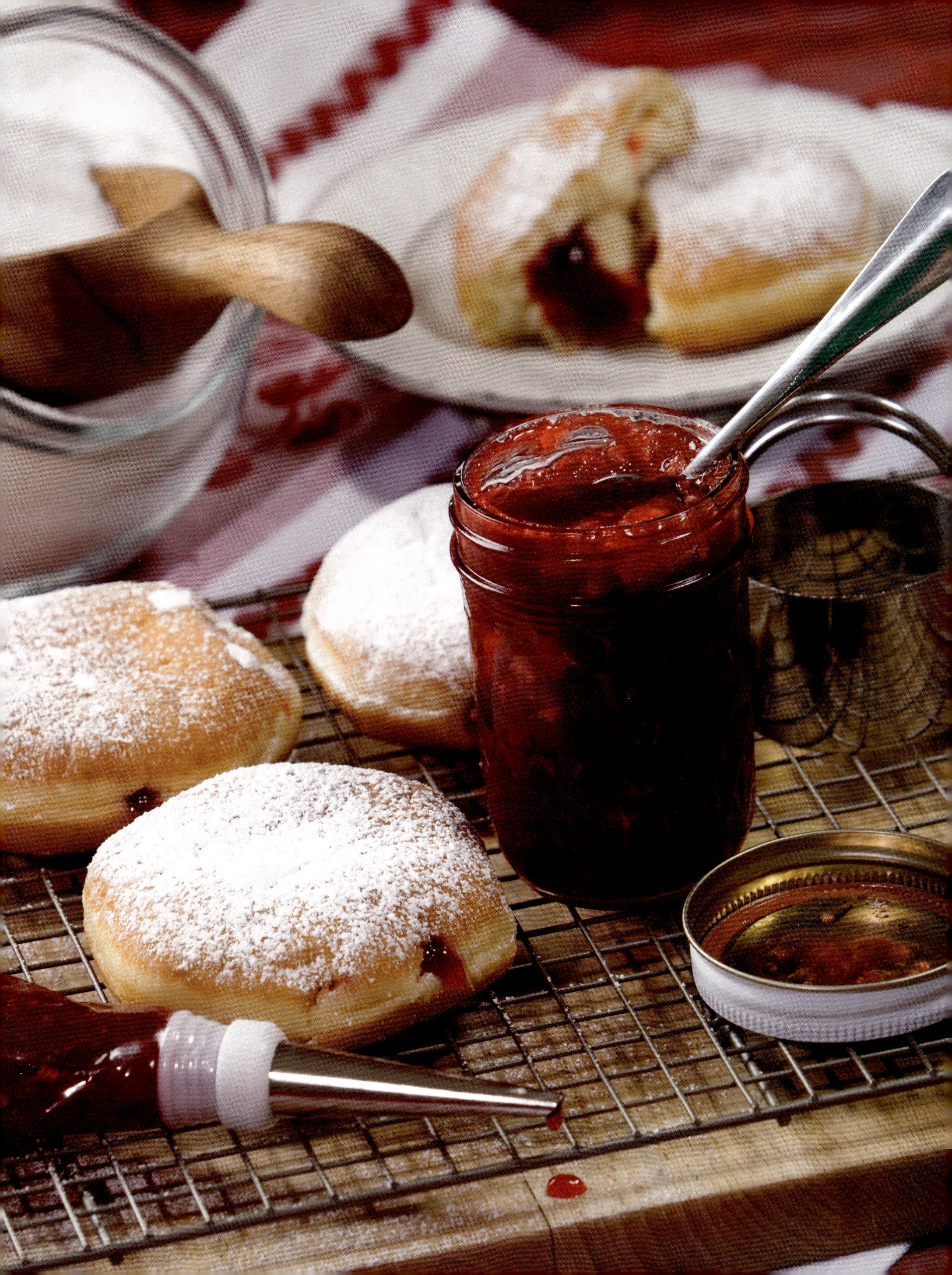

Pretty Peach Preserves

Makes 4 cups

Ingredients

2 cups chunky peach puree, made from 2 pounds fresh peaches
½ teaspoon citric acid
3¾ cups granulated sugar
1 pouch (3 ounces) liquid fruit pectin

Peaches are one of my husband's favorite fruit and when I first made this jam for him, he could not believe that this jam was not only delicious, but so easy to make. We went peach picking the next day and he made a batch by himself. He loves to sneak a spoonful, straight from the jar as a late night "sweet tooth" fix. My family enjoys this jam best served on hot butter biscuits.

1. Place all ingredients in the order listed into the bread maker; stir until sugar is moistened and close the lid.

2. Press MENU and select JAM.

3. Press START (unit will heat for 15 minutes before paddles start turning).

4. Total machine time is 1 hour and 20 minutes.

Marian's Tip:
Store in jars in the refrigerator for up to 3 months or in the freezer for up to 1 year.

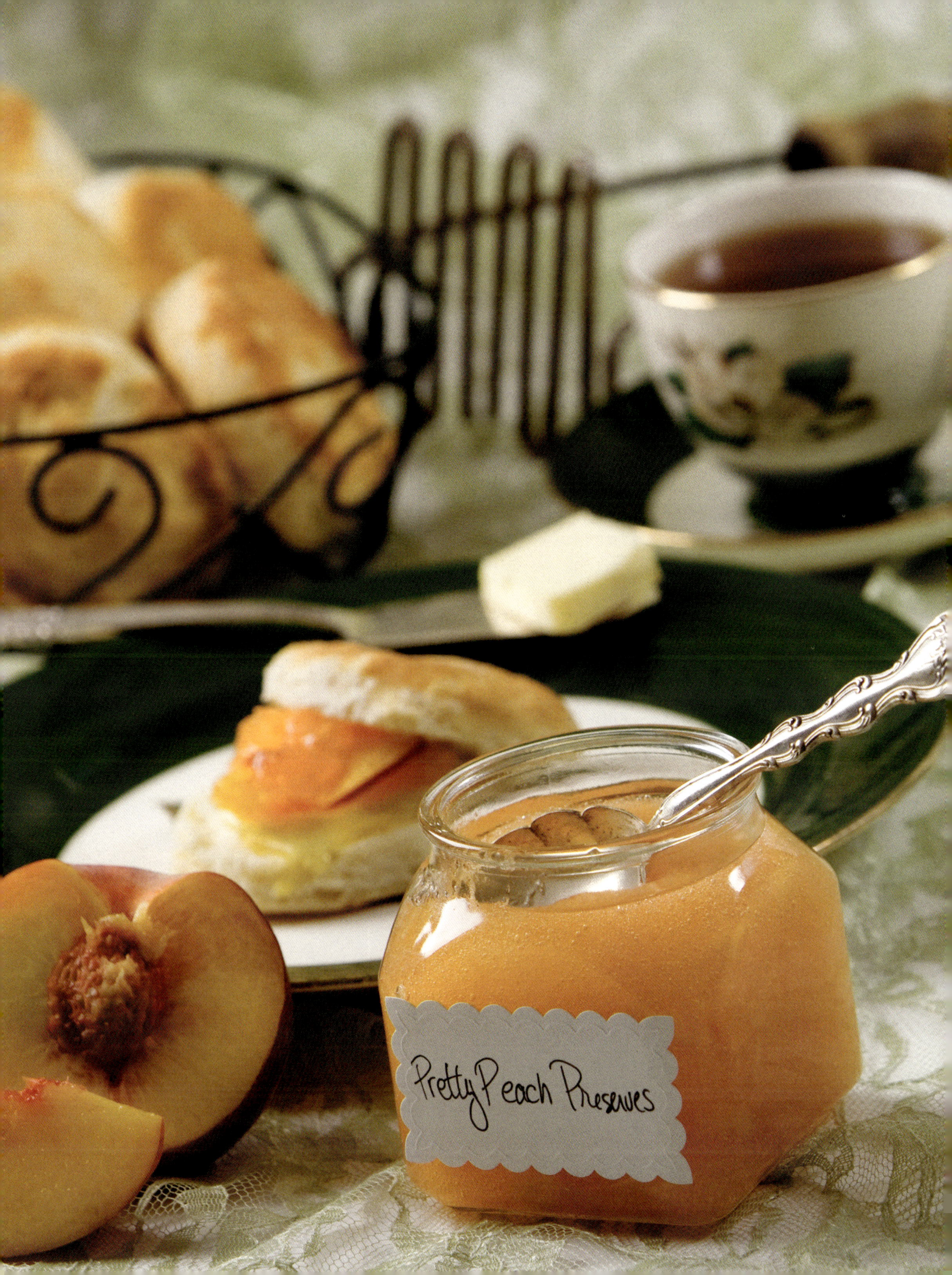
Pretty Peach Preserves

Harvest Pear Jam

Makes 4 cups

Ingredients

2 cups chunky pear puree, made from 4 large ripe pears, unpeeled
¾ teaspoon citric acid or 2 tablespoons fresh lemon juice
3½ cups granulated sugar
1 pouch (3 ounces) liquid fruit pectin

Although pears make excellent jam, very rarely will you find this fruit made into any type of preserve at grocery stores. This is all the more reason to make some in your bread maker. You can use any kind of pears you like as long as they are ripe and very fragrant.

1. Place all ingredients in the order listed into the bread maker; stir until sugar is moistened and close the lid.

2. Press MENU and select JAM.

3. Press START (unit will heat for 15 minutes before paddles start turning).

4. Total machine time is 1 hour and 20 minutes.

Marian's Tip:
Store in jars in the refrigerator for up to 3 months or in the freezer for up to 1 year.

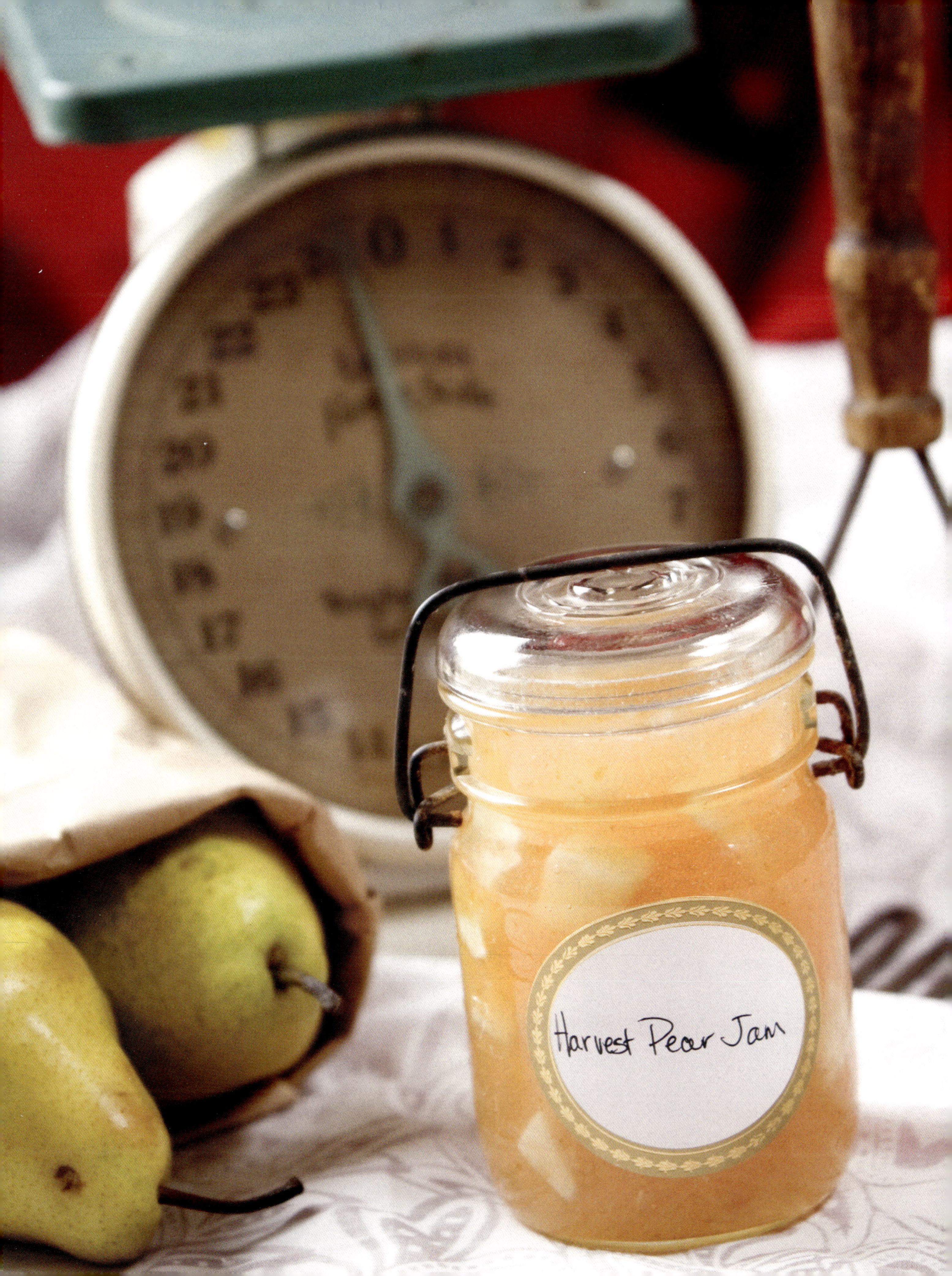
Harvest Pear Jam

Pretty Plum Preserves

Makes 4 cups

Ingredients

2 cups chunky plum puree, made from 2 pounds fresh, unpeeled purple plums
3¾ cups granulated sugar
1 pouch (3 ounces) liquid fruit pectin

No one needs to know how easy this recipe is to make. In the past, I have made jams and jellies the hard way, using pots on the stove and jars going in and out of the canning pot. Nowadays, I still want the charm and exquisite taste of homemade canned items, but I don't need to preserve the harvest the way that I did when I was younger.

1. Place all ingredients in the order listed into the bread maker; stir until sugar is moistened and close the lid.

2. Press MENU and select JAM.

3. Press START (unit will heat for 15 minutes before paddles start turning).

4. Total machine time is 1 hour and 20 minutes.

Marian's Tip:
I use my immersion blender to puree the plums.

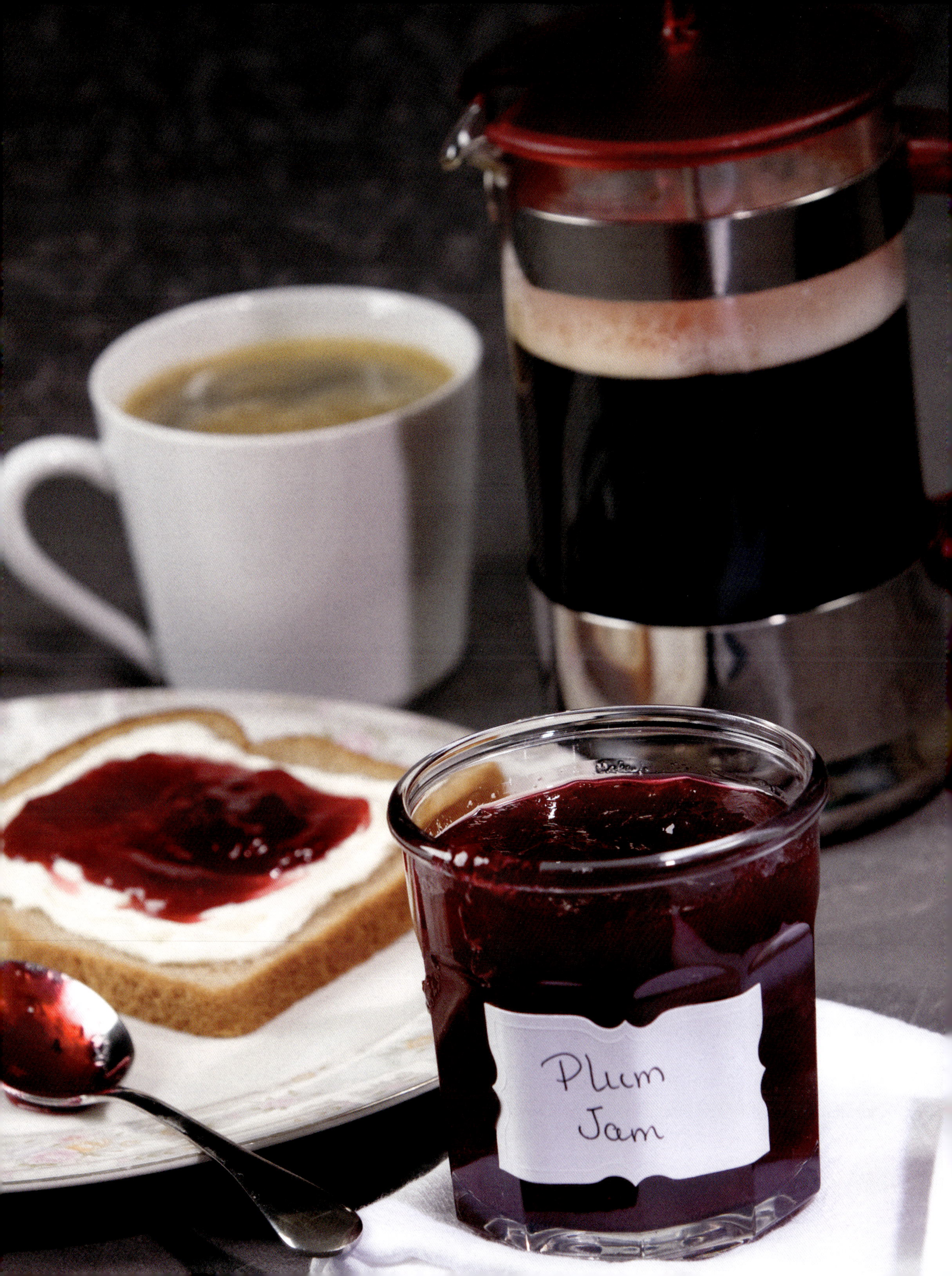
Plum
Jam

Florida Tangerine Marmalade

Makes 4 cups

Ingredients

1½ cups tangerine pulp, made from whole tangerines, finely ground in a food processor
3 cups granulated sugar
1 box (1.75 ounces) dry fruit pectin

As a child, making marmalade was an all-day process. After picking the fruit, we peeled it, scraped it, sliced the rinds and boiled them. Next, we squeezed the juice and carefully gathered the seeds to tie them up in a cheesecloth bag, which we added to the pot (these provide lots of natural pectin). Then, we cooked it in a kettle on an old, cast iron wood burning stove. We stirred it with a wooden paddle until it was thick. Finally, we canned it so that we could enjoy that delicious marmalade for many months. While I miss my years in Africa, with the long days and slow progress (courtesy of a lack of electricity), I love my life in Florida even more. In this fast-paced day and age, it is wonderful to whirr local citrus fruit in my food processor for a few seconds, put it into my bread machine, and make hands-free marmalade to enjoy with my whole day still intact. Making this jam with tangerines instead of oranges is a delightful change of taste with all the great qualities of the marmalade still present.

1. Place all ingredients in the order listed into the bread maker; stir until sugar is moistened and close the lid.

2. Press MENU and select JAM.

3. Press START (unit will heat for 15 minutes before paddles start turning).

4. Total machine time is 1 hour and 20 minutes.

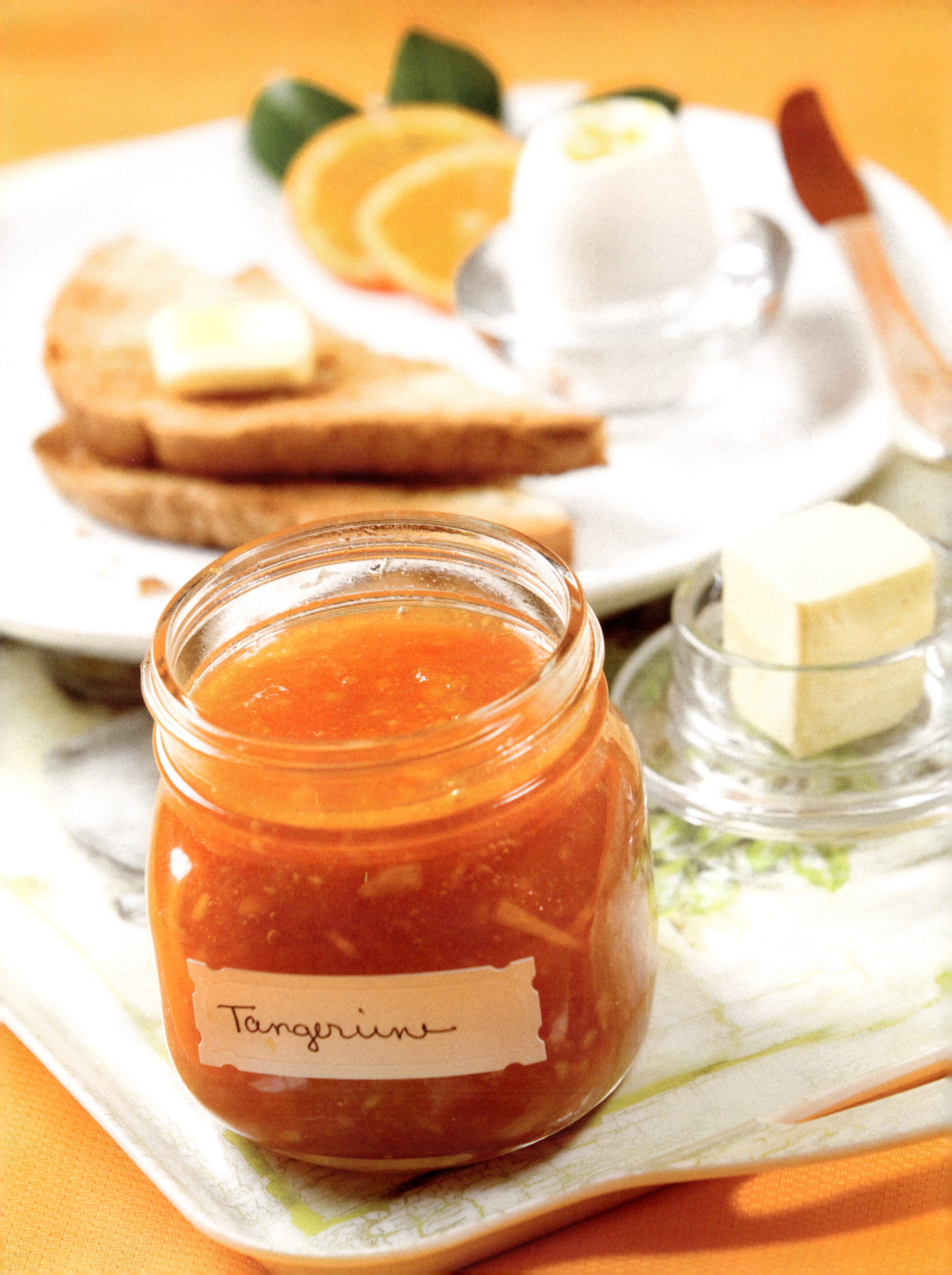
Tangerine

Kiwi Jam

Makes 4 cups

Ingredients

2 cups fresh and chunky kiwi puree, made from 8 peeled, ripe kiwi berries
½ teaspoon citric acid or 1 tablespoon fresh lemon juice
3½ cups granulated sugar
1 pouch (3 ounces) liquid fruit pectin

Have you ever seen kiwi jam at your grocery store? Although it is a very delicious jam, you won't find this sweet/tart jam readily available. It is so pretty with the flecks from the black seeds and its very nice green color. This kiwi jam also tastes great on thumb-print cookies. It is Ben's favorite jam and I often tuck a jar of it into a care package and mail it off to him at college.

1. Place all ingredients in the order listed into the bread maker; stir until sugar is moistened and close the lid.

2. Press MENU and select JAM.

3. Press START (unit will heat for 15 minutes before paddles start turning).

4. Total machine time is 1 hour and 20 minutes.

Marian's Tip:
   Store in jars in the refrigerator for up to 3 months or in the freezer for up to 1 year.

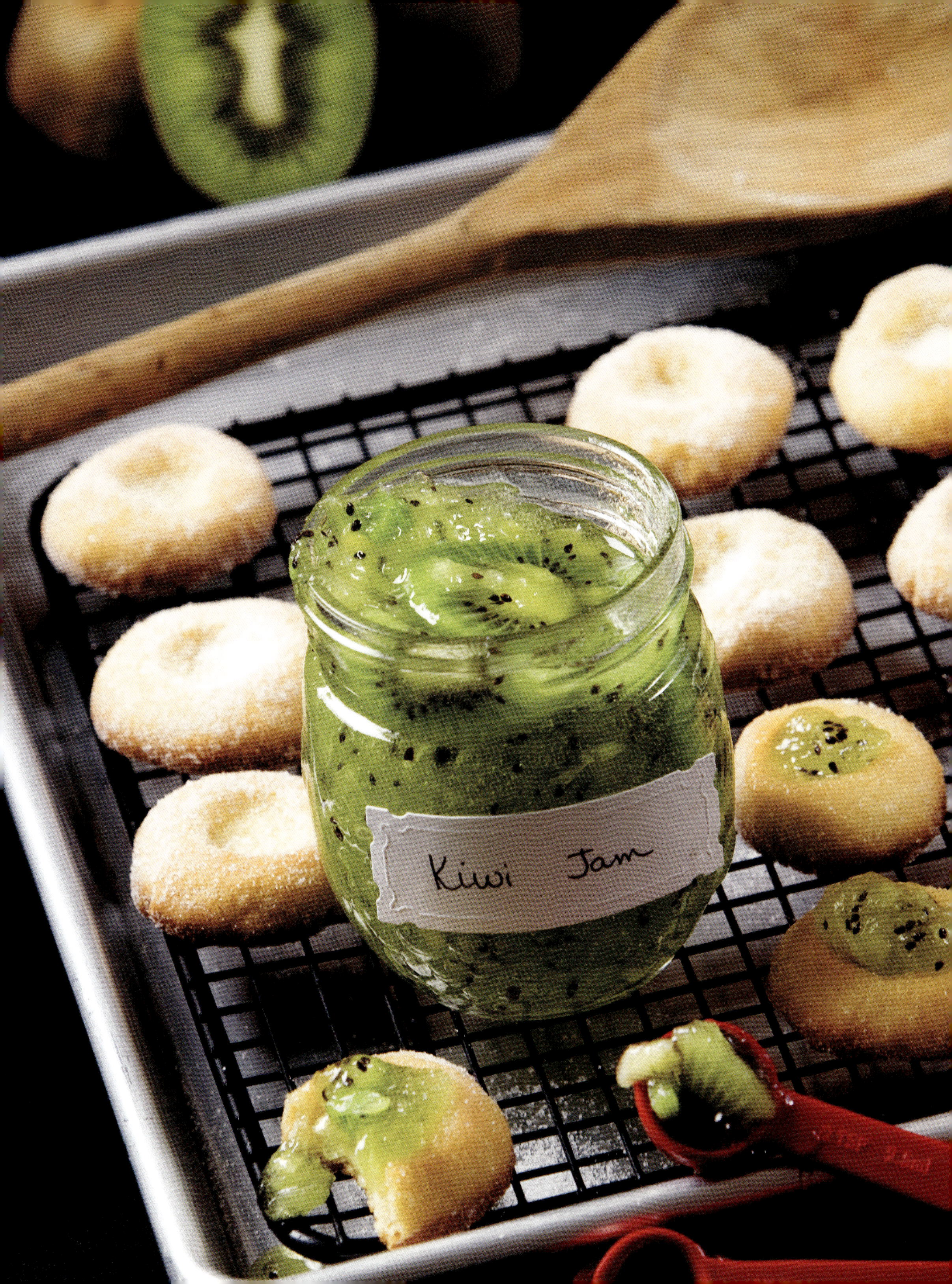
Kiwi Jam

Lemon Curd

Makes 3 cups

Ingredients

¾ cup granulated sugar
¾ cup (1½ sticks) unsalted butter, softened
1 tablespoon lemon zest
¾ cup fresh lemon juice
6 egg yolks, whisked

When I discovered that the bread maker's JAM setting could turn out perfect lemon curd, it made my day. Lemon curd has a bright, clean flavor, both sweet and tart. It is great on a piece of toast, on biscuits, as a filling for cakes and cookies or enjoyed by the spoonful straight from the jar. The mixture thickens into a silky mass because of the reaction between the acid in the lemon, sugar and egg yolks. Since it freezes well, I always keep a stash of it my freezer.

1. Place all ingredients, except egg yolks into the bread maker; close lid.

2. Press MENU and select JAM.

3. Press START (unit will heat for 15 minutes before paddles start turning).

4. When paddles start turning after 15 minutes, add egg yolks to the bread maker; close lid.

5. Total machine time is 1 hour and 20 minutes.

6. Strain lemon curd through a fine mesh strainer.

7. You can store this lemon curd in jars in the refrigerator for 2 weeks or in the freezer for up to 2 months.

Marian's Tip:
You can easily turn this into lime or grapefruit curd by switching the lemon juice and zest for lime or grapefruit juice and zest. Just remember to zest before juicing to make it easier. You can add a few drops of food coloring to brighten up the color.

Lemon Curd

Hot Red Pepper Jelly

Makes about 4 cups

Ingredients

½ cup jalapeno peppers, seeded, deribbed and finely diced
½ cup red bell pepper, seeded and finely diced
½ cup green bell pepper, seeded and finely diced
¾ cup apple cider vinegar
3¼ cups granulated sugar
1 pouch (3 ounces) liquid fruit pectin

A dear friend of mine from Louisiana taught me how to make this jelly. In Louisiana, they like to serve it poured over the top of Creole cream cheese. It is also delicious served as an appetizer with crackers. The amber color and pretty flecks of red and green from the peppers, is simply gorgeous. However, unless you are accustomed to the heat of chilies on your fingers, wear gloves when cutting up the jalapenos.

1. Place all ingredients in the order listed into the bread maker; close lid.

2. Press MENU and select JAM.

3. Press START.

4. Total machine time is 1 hour and 20 minutes.

Mango Chutney

Makes 1 loaf

Ingredients

2 ripe mangoes, peeled and diced into ½-inch cubes
1 cup raisins
1 yellow onion, peeled and chopped
3 garlic cloves, minced
2 tablespoons fresh ginger, peeled and minced
½ cup apple cider vinegar
2½ cups granulated sugar
1 tablespoon kosher salt
1 teaspoon curry powder
1 teaspoon turmeric
1 teaspoon red pepper flakes
1 tablespoon coriander seed
1 pouch (3 ounces) liquid fruit pectin

I love all things pickled and chutney, with its complex flavors and textures, is one of my favorite condiments. I sneak it into many of my recipes and I truly enjoy it on a simple ham sandwich. This version is my take on a recipe that one of my childhood friend's mom used to make.

1. Place all ingredients in the order listed into the bread maker; stir until sugar is moistened and close the lid.

2. Press MENU and select JAM.

3. Press START (unit will heat for 15 minutes before paddles start turning).

4. Total machine time is 1 hour and 20 minutes.

Rhubarb Jam

Makes 4 cups

Ingredients

2¼ cups fresh rhubarb, finely chopped
½ cup water
3 cups granulated sugar
1 pouch (3 ounces) liquid fruit pectin

Rhubarb, while actually a vegetable, is almost always treated like a fruit. It is one of the first fruits to appear in the spring. Its tartness is delightful when paired with things that are sweet. If your rhubarb has any leaves on the stalks, be sure to cut and discard them because they contain oxalic acid, which is toxic. The pretty red stalks do not contain this acid. I love sweets made with rhubarb. This jam really allows its subtle flavor to shine through.

1. Place rhubarb and water into a microwave safe bowl; microwave on high for 7 minutes or until rhubarb is soft and tender.

2. Transfer rhubarb to bread maker.

3. Add sugar and pectin to bread maker; stir until sugar is moistened and close the lid.

4. Press MENU and select JAM.

5. Press START (unit will heat for 15 minutes before paddles start turning).

6. Total machine time is 1 hour and 20 minutes.

Source Page

Here are some of my favorite places to find ingredients, supplies and tools that are not readily available at grocery stores.

Chocolatesource.com
9 Crest Road
Wellesley, MA 02482
800-214-4269
www.chocolatecource.com
My favorite Callebaut cocoa

Chocosphere
P.O. Box 2237
Tualatin, OR 97062
877-992-4623
www.chocosphere.com
*Excellent quality cocoa such as Callebaut
All Chocolates
Jimmies and sprinkles*

**The Bakers Catalogue at
King Arthur Flour**
135 Route 5 South
P.O. Box 1010
Norwich, VT 05055
www.kingarthurflour.com
*Flours, tools, pure orange, lemon,
lime oils, Fiori Di Sicilia oil, citric acid,
diastatic malt powder,
vital wheat gluten, lecithin,
powdered milk, rubber spatulas*

**Sweet Celebrations
(Formerly Maid Of Scandinavia)**
7009 Washington Ave. S.
Edina, MN 55439
800-328-6722
www.sweetc.com
Cake decorating supplies and much more

Colorado State University
Toll free 1-877-692-9358
Cerc1@ur.colostate.edu
High altitude baking guides

Penzeys Spices
P.O. Box 924
Brookfield, WI 53045
800-741-7787
www.penzeys.com
Spices, extracts and more

Gluten-Free Mall
4927 Sonoma HWY Suite C1
Santa Rosa, CA 95409
707-509-4528
www.glutenfreemall.com
All ingredients needed for gluten-free baking

D & G Occasions
625 Herndon Ave.
Orlando, FL 32803
407-894-4458
www.dandgoccasions.com
*My favorite butter vanilla extract by Magic Line,
cake and candy making supplies, citric acid*

**Vanilla From Tahiti
Nui Enterprises**
501 Chapala St. Suite A
Santa Barbara, CA 93101
805-965-5153
www.vanillafromtahiti.com
*My favorite pure vanilla extract and
vanilla beans*

Whole Foods
550 Bowie St.
Austin, TX 78703
512-477-4455
www.wholefoods.com
*Grains, such as teff, spelt, citric acid,
xanthan gum, 100% whole wheat flour*

Index

A
All-American Hamburger Buns 34
All-American Wheat Bread 16
Altitudes, Higher 8
Apple Sauce Quick Bread 84

B
Billowy Seven Minute Frosting 103
Blueberry Lemon Quick Bread 74
Brioche 13
Brown Butter 57
Brown Butter Sandwich Bread 56

Banana
My Favorite Banana Bread 72

Brownies
Jordan & Ben's Brownies 82

Buns
All-American Hamburger Buns 34

Butter
Brown Butter 57
Easy Anytime Apple Butter 135

Buttercrust
Home Style Buttercrust Bread 22

C
Carrot Cake 86
Challah 24
Chocolate Crazy Cake 108
Chocolate Ganache Icing 96
Chocolaty Yeast Bread 65
Chili Cheese Bread 32
Cinnamon Raisin Bread 60
Citric Acid 7
Classic Pound Cake 97
Coconut Cake 88
Coconut Cake Frosting 90
Coconut Yeast Bread 62
Confetti Veggie Bread 48
Cranberry Orange Quick Bread 76

Cake
Carrot Cake 86
Chocolate Crazy Cake 108
Classic Pound Cake 97
Coconut Cake 88
Easy Moist Chocolate Cake 104
Easy Vanilla Yellow Cake 92
Glazed Cream Cheese Pound Cake 98
My Favorite Chocolate Pound Cake 102
Oatmeal Cake 94
Southern Red Velvet Cake 110
Sticky Toffee Pudding Cake 91
Wolf's Lemon Pound Cake 100

Cheese
Chili Cheese Bread 32
Easy Very Cheesy Bread 33

Chive
Sour Cream & Chive Bread 47

Corn Bread
Extra Corny Corn Bread 67
Mama Claire's Spoon Bread 69

D
Diastatic Malt Powder 7

Dough
All-American Hamburger Buns 34
Wolf's Pizza Dough 51

E
Easiest White Sandwich Bread 14
Easy Anytime Apple Butter 135
Easy Moist Chocolate Cake 104
Easy Vanilla Yellow Cake 92
Easy Very Cheesy Bread 33
English Muffin Bread 28
Extra Corny Corn Bread 67

F
Focaccia Bread 40
French Bread 30
French Bread with Sourdough Starter 44

Frosting
Billowy Seven Minute Frosting 103
Chocolate Ganache Icing 96
Coconut Cake Frosting 90
Southern Red Velvet Cake Icing 112

G
Gingerbread Cake 81
Glazed Cream Cheese Pound Cake 98
Glaze For Chocolate Crazy Cake 107

Ganache
Chocolate Ganache Icing 96

Glazes
Chocolate Ganache Icing 96
Cream Cheese Pound Cake Glaze 98
Glaze For Chocolate Crazy Cake 107
Lemon Glaze 100

Gluten-Free
Gluten-Free, About 9
Gluten-Free Banana Bread 126
Gluten-Free Brownies 132
Gluten-Free Buttercrust Bread 122
Gluten-Free Chocolate Pound Cake 130
Gluten-Free Corn Bread 124
Gluten-Free Garlic Herb Bread 116
Gluten-Free Pizza Dough 120
Gluten-Free Rice Bread 118

Gluten-Free Stuffing Bread 123
Gluten-Free Zucchini Bread 128
My Favorite Gluten-Free Bread 114

Grain
Seven Grain Bread 20
Whole Grain Oatmeal Bread 54

H
Hawaiian Sweet Bread 64
Home Style Buttercrust Bread 22

I

Icing
Billowy Seven Minute Frosting 103
Chocolate Ganache Icing 96
Coconut Cake Frosting 90
Southern Red Velvet Cake Icing 112

Italian
Pepperoni Pizza Bread 50

J
Jordan & Ben's Brownies 82

Jams, Jellies & More
Easy Anytime Apple Butter 135
Florida Tangerine Marmalade 148
Greg's Favorite Blueberry Jam 138
Harvest Pear Jam 144
Homemade Strawberry Jelly 136
Hot Red Pepper Jelly 154
Kiwi Jam 150
Lemon Curd 152
Mango Chutney 155
Michigan Tart Red Cherry Jam 140
Pretty Peach Preserves 142
Pretty Plum Preserves 146
Rhubarb Jam 156

K
Kalamata Olive Sourdough Bread 36
Kansas Sunflower Seed Bread 38

L

Lemon
Blueberry Lemon Quick Bread 74
Wolf's Lemon Pound Cake 100
Lemon Glaze 100

M
Mama Claire's Spoon Bread 69
Measurements 10
My Favorite Banana Bread 72
My Favorite Chocolate Pound Cake 102

Muffin
English Muffin Bread 28

Mushroom
Savory Mushroom Bread 46

N

Nuts
Pistachio Nut Bread 58

O
Old Fashioned Rye Bread 45
Onion & Sage White Bread 41

Oatmeal
Whole Grain Oatmeal Bread 54

Olive
Kalamata Olive Sourdough Bread 36

Orange
Cranberry Orange Quick Bread 76

P
Pepperoni Pizza Bread 50
Pistachio Nut Bread 58
Poppyseed Bread 68
Powdered Milk, About 7
Pumpernickel Bread 26
Pumpkin Bread 80

Pizza
Pepperoni Pizza Bread 50
Wolf's Pizza Dough 51

Potato
Sweet Potato Bread 55

Pudding
Sticky Toffee Pudding Cake 91

Pumpernickel
Pumpernickel Bread 26

Q

Quick Breads
Apple Sauce Quick Bread 84
Blueberry Lemon Quick Bread 74
Cranberry Orange Quick Bread 76
Extra Corny Corn Bread 67
Gingerbread Cake 81
Jordan & Ben's Brownies 82
Mama Claire's Spoon Bread 69
My Favorite Banana Bread 72
Poppyseed Bread 68
Pumpkin Bread 80
Sour Cream Coffee Cake 78
Zucchini Bread 70

R

Removing Bread From The Pan 8

Raisin
Cinnamon Raisin Bread 60

Rye
Old Fashioned Rye Bread 45

S

Salt, About 6
Savory Mushroom Bread 46
Seven Grain Bread 20
Sour Cream & Chive Bread 47
Sour Cream Coffee Cake 78
Sourdough Starter 43
Sourdough Teff Bread 42
Southern Red Velvet Cake 110
Southern Red Velvet Cake Icing 112
Sticky Toffee Pudding Cake 91

Sage
Onion & Sage White Bread 41

Sandwich
Brown Butter Sandwich Bread 56
Easiest White Sandwich Bread 14

Sourdough
French Bread with Sourdough Starter 44
Kalamata Olive Sourdough Bread 36
Sourdough Teff Bread 42

Spoon Bread
Mama Claire's Spoon Bread 69

T

Thanksgiving Bread 53
Troubleshooting 10

Teff
Sourdough Teff Bread 42

V

Vital Wheat Gluten, About 6

Vanilla
Easy Vanilla Yellow Cake 92
Vanilla, About 6

Vegetable
Confetti Veggie Bread 48

W

Wild Rice Bread 52
Wolf's Lemon Pound Cake 100
Wolf's Pizza Dough 51

Wheat
100% Whole Wheat Bread 18
All-American Wheat Bread 16

White
Easiest White Sandwich Bread 14
Home Style Buttercrust Bread 22
Onion & Sage White Bread 41

Whole Grain
Seven Grain Bread 20
Whole Grain Oatmeal Bread 54

Y

Yeast, About 7

Z

Zucchini Bread 70